Fashions of a Decade The 1990s

Fashions of a Decade The 1990s

Anne McEvoy

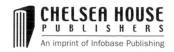

CHELSEA HOUSE PUBLISHERS
An imprint of Infobase Publishing

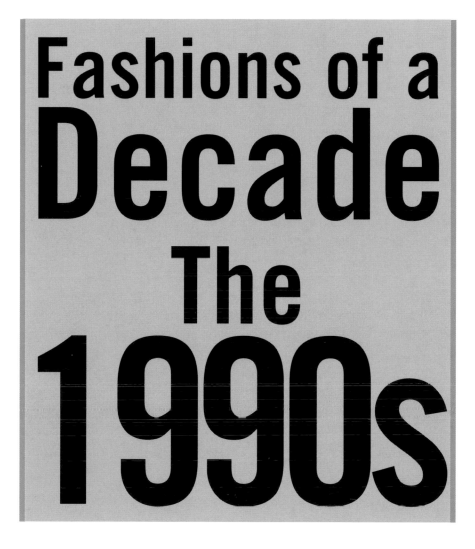

Chelsea House
An imprint of Infobase Publishing
132 West 31st Street
New York NY 10001

For Library of Congress Cataloging-in-Publication Data please contact the publisher.
ISBN-13: 978-0-8160-6725-1
ISBN-10: 0-8160-6725-2

Research for new edition: Kathy Elgin
Editor: Karen Taschek
Text design by Simon Borrough
Cover design by Dorothy M. Preston
Illustrations by Robert Price
Picture Research by Shelley Noronha

This new edition produced for Chelsea House by Bailey Publishing Associates Ltd.

Printed in China through Morris Press, Ltd.

Bang EJB 10 9 8 7 6 5 4 3 2

This book is printed on acid-free paper.

Contents

The 1990s

▲ As the Communist empire disintegrated, statues of Lenin were removed from public display in most of the countries of Eastern Europe, marking the end of an era.

▼ American and Allied forces, victorious in the Gulf War, hardly suspected that their desert-issue gear would start a new fashion craze back home.

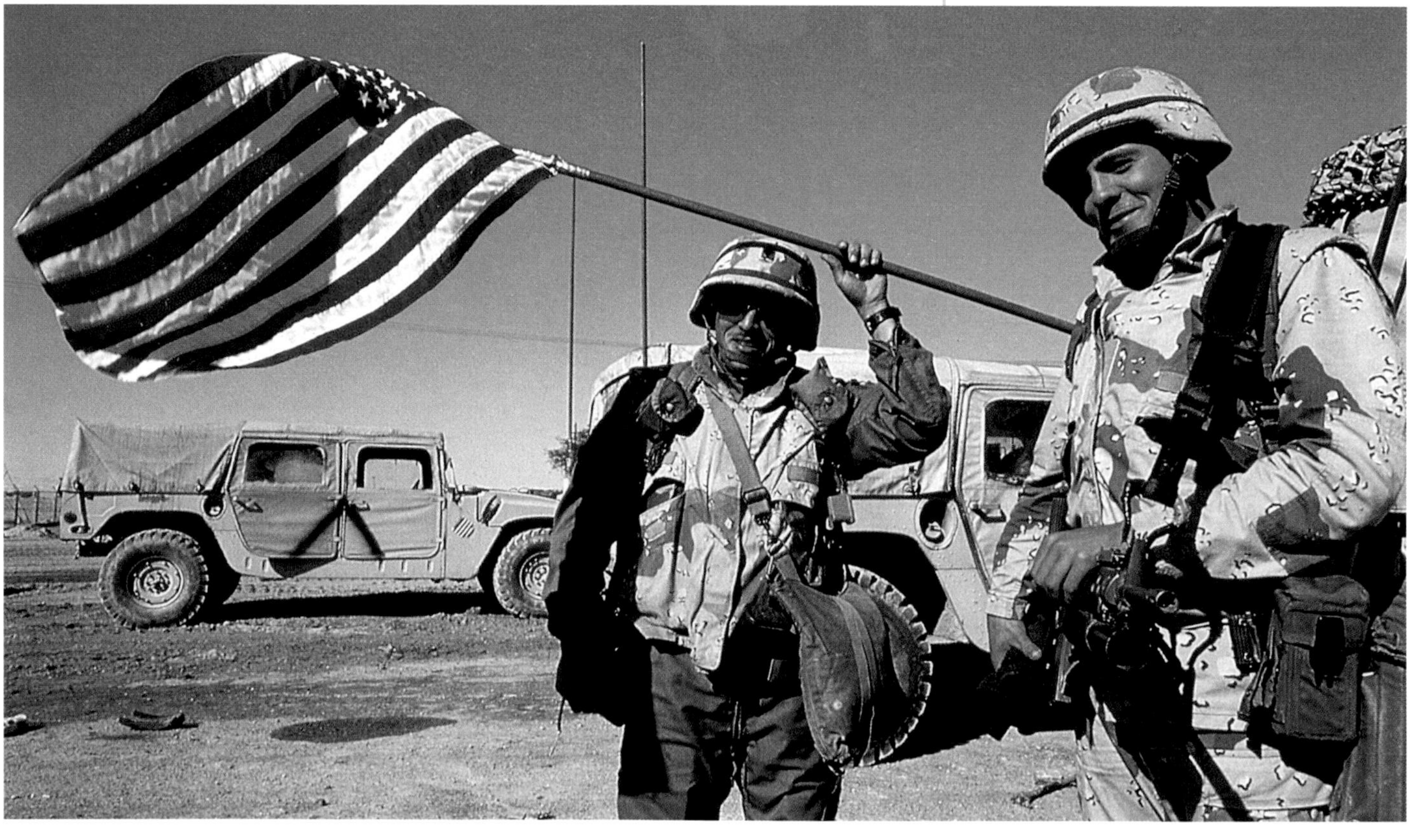

As the end of the twentieth century finally came in sight, the world experienced a crisis of turmoil and rapid change. Seemingly impossible things happened. The unshakable Soviet Union fell apart, creating great political upheaval, long-established leaders were overthrown, old borders disappeared, and new alliances were forged.

The pace of life accelerated sharply. Technology was developing at whirlwind speed, and we depended on it more and more for communication, business, and entertainment. The Internet, mobile phones, personal organizers, and other gadgets—still something of a

The End of Communism

In 1991, reforms begun by Mikhail Gorbachev in the late eighties culminated in what few people had believed possible: the breakup of the Soviet Union and, effectively, the end of Communism.

In early 1991, faced with separatist unrest in several of the Soviet states, Gorbachev attempted to restructure the USSR. More radical reformers, however, believed that a swift transition to a market economy was needed, even if it meant the disintegration of the Soviet Union. In August, hard-line Communists launched a coup against President Gorbachev, who was held under house arrest in Crimea. The coup did not gain public support, however, and thousands took to the streets to protest. President Gorbachev returned to Moscow, but his powers were fatally undermined, and on December 25, he resigned. By the end of the month, the Soviet flag was lowered for the last time over the Kremlin, and the USSR ceased to exist. Eleven of the fifteen former states of the USSR formed the new Confederation of Independent States (CIS). Worldwide headlines hailed the dismantling of the entire structure of Soviet Communism.

After the collapse of the Soviet Union, democratic movements swept across much of Eastern Europe. One after another, states freed themselves from almost half a century of Communist rule.

novelty in the eighties—became essential parts of everyday life.

For some, it was a grim time. The threat of terrorist attack intensified worldwide, and individual acts of terrible violence took place. Although the Cold War was over, conflicts continued to ravage many parts of the world, from Asia to Central America, from Africa to the Balkans and, perhaps most threateningly, the Middle East. For those in the former Soviet states, however, it was a thrilling time. Making the most of their new-found freedom and capitalist economies, they were eager for the luxury goods denied them for so long, and that included fashionable clothing. A huge new market was opening up, but that meant competition, too.

The sense of change in the world order was reflected in a restless and unsettled social scene in which people moved around more, changed jobs more frequently, and divorced more easily. And, as ever, fashion proved a mirror to the world.

◀ Demonstrators against the hard-line Communist coup were stirred by a memorable speech made by Boris Yeltsin from the turret of a tank in front of the Russian White House. The surrounding troops eventually defected and most of the coup leaders fled.

The Way We Wore

The 1990s have been called the decade of anti-fashion, the decade when street fashion finally won out over haute couture, and the decade that saw the death of the designer. In a way, these descriptions were all correct, but the 1990s could just as easily be called the decade of "fashions," plural. The term "anything goes" had never been more correct.

The opening years of the 1990s saw a predictable backlash against the power dressing of the eighties, but this did not result in any single, new defining style for the new decade. The nineties were a magpie decade, picking and combining from any style or period that appealed. Nostalgia and retro were high on the agenda: often, it seemed that a trend had hardly passed before it was being revived, given an ironic makeover, and put back on the runway. New, avant-garde designers revisited earlier periods and presented their own collections as homages or updates.

This readiness to cannibalize other styles led to the charge that the real creative intelligence had gone out of fashion. There were more labels and more star names than ever before. But were they really designers, or just slick masters of pastiche who knew how to reinterpret existing ideas for a new, consumer-driven market? As the decade progressed, the charge became more difficult to deny, but consumers didn't seem to care—and neither did many of the designers. Italian Franco Moschino, whose company profile soared during the nineties, readily owned up to the charge. "Fashion," he said, "is now anybody you want it to be."

▲ The emerging Italian partnership of Dolce and Gabbana had a typically flamboyant take on the sixties revival, as seen in this patchwork hippie outfit from 1993.

A Violent Decade

It seemed that violence was becoming a feature of everyday life. In February 1993, seventy-six followers of the Branch Davidian cult led by David Koresh died in a mass suicide after a siege at their compound in Waco, Texas. In March 1996, in Dunblane, Scotland, a gunman shot himself after killing or injuring all but one of a class of twenty-nine five- and six-year-olds at the local primary school. This was just the first in a spate of school shootings. America's worst came in April 1999, when two teenagers at Columbine High School in Colorado shot dead twelve fellow students and a teacher and wounded twenty-four others before themselves committing suicide. At least fourteen more school shootings followed in the next few months, provoking debate about gun control laws and the availability of firearms, particularly in the United States. Many also questioned the role of violent movies and video games in Western society.

Racial tensions also exploded in violence. In 1992, riots exploded in Los Angeles when four white policemen were acquitted of assault charges after beating up a black motorist, Rodney King. And in 1995, a real-life courtroom drama was played out on television. After a spectacular car chase, African-American football hero O. J. Simpson went on trial for the murder of his ex-wife, Nicole, and her companion, Ron Goldman. The trial, and Simpson's acquittal, divided America along racial lines.

▲ As rioting broke out in Los Angeles over the Rodney King affair, whole areas of the city were devastated by several days of burning and looting.

►A young girl plants thirteen symbolic crosses—one for each of the twelve students and a teacher—along with the flowers and other gifts at the Columbine memorial. Informal memorial sites like this, with flowers, candles, toys, and messages left by well-wishers, were a growing public response to the many violent events and tragic deaths of the nineties.

▲ **On the fashion runway, a political platform, or an outdoor radio broadcast, DKNY cool established your credentials as someone worth listening to.**

Slowing Down in the Fast Lane

The nineties opened with economic recession and high unemployment figures. For many, the previous decade's freewheeling spending came to a screeching halt. Even among those less affected by recession, the "greed is good" slogan of the high-achieving eighties gave way to a more serious attitude toward life and work. The yuppies were aging out. Ambitious young executives now had to work long hours for their high salaries. The idea of a job for life became a thing of the past. People moved from one job to another after only a year or two or combined several strands of employment in what became known as a "portfolio career."

Terrorism

The threat of global terrorism became a reality in the nineties. America had its first taste of horror in February 1993, when a bomb was planted under the World Trade Center in New York. Perhaps more shocking, however, was the bombing of the Federal Building in Oklahoma City on April 19, 1995. This time it turned out that the person responsible was not a foreign terrorist but US army veteran and anti-government extremist Timothy McVeigh. The explosion killed 167 and injured hundreds more. The 1996 Olympic Games were given a dramatic start when a bomb went off during a concert in Atlanta's Centennial Olympic Park, killing one person and injuring over a hundred. American interests overseas were also at risk: an explosion at the US embassy in Nairobi, Kenya, in August 1999 killed 250 and injured 5,000.

In Northern Ireland, a society long used to terrorist atrocity saw its single worst incident on August 15, 1998, when an IRA bomb in the small town of Omagh killed twenty-nine people and injured 200, most of them families enjoying Saturday shopping. In Israel, the Palestinian campaign saw an upsurge in the number of terrorist attacks by suicide bombers who chose to blow themselves up on buses or in restaurants, taking with them as many innocent bystanders as possible. This technique spread quickly to other conflict zones and in the following decade would be a major weapon in the terrorist arsenal.

With little time to spare in their busy lives, people demanded more instant gratification. Shopping patterns changed, with more shopping done on the Internet. Having worked hard for their money, people wanted their purchases to define them as successful people. Logos and brands became all-important. People did not seem to mind being used as walking advertisements but happily bought into the deal. A plain black T-shirt with DKNY on it said everything: you were worth it.

The End of Couture?

Recession hit the major European fashion houses hard. With less money to spend, people rejected short-lived designer fashions in favor of more economical ready-to-wear lines. This was especially true in America, which had traditionally accounted for 40 percent of the couture business. Paris felt the shock waves: in 1992, veteran designer Yves Saint Laurent declared in *Le Figaro* that haute couture would not survive the decade.

The major houses realized that in order to survive, they had to diversify and attract a younger clientele. They fought back by absorbing the street fashion of youth culture and feeding it back to the streets—with a high price tag. Just like the punk movement of the seventies, radical styles may have originated on the streets but were swiftly taken over and managed by the professionals. This saved the major design houses—and changed the face of fashion completely.

Diffusion Is the Difference

Hardly anyone could actually afford to buy the serious couture styles. Even the ready-to-wear styles, which brought in most of the income, were beyond the reach of the average shopper. In the cash-strapped nineties, savvy design directors extended their reach in two ways.

First, they developed lines of accessories that, although not necessarily produced by them, carried their name. Perfume and sunglasses were the major items, but shoes, purses, and costume jewelry soon followed. Easily identified by the prominent logo, these items had cachet. Even if you couldn't afford the clothes, you could buy into the dream with a carefully chosen accessory.

Designers also reached out to the new consumer by developing "diffusion" collections, so called because they diffuse the essence of the designer's style for a mass market. Diffusion clothes retain the quality of cut and finish associated with a design house but are usually made from less expensive fabrics and sell for about half the price of standard ready-to-wear. American designer Michael Kors summed up the philosophy: "Just because a woman doesn't have the pocketbook doesn't mean she doesn't have style."

One after another, designers announced diffusion collections: John Galliano launched "Galliano Girl" in 1991, and Moschino came right to the point with the "Cheap & Chic" label. The prime example is designer-manufacturer Donna Karan, hailed as "the Princess of 7th Avenue" (the New York City street central to the garment trade). Her DKNY range embraces sunglasses, watches, swimwear, jeans, perfume, and home linens alongside upmarket, affordable clothing for men, women, and children.

Easy, Man

Dress codes were abandoned as dress-down Friday fashions gradually took over the rest of the week. Chinos or khakis, denim shirts and polos, and a casual linen jacket now made up the average man's working wardrobe. Similar collections of separates filled women's closets. Jeans became acceptable virtually everywhere for both sexes, from workplace to exclusive art gallery openings, dressed up with a tailored jacket and jewelry. Depending on the year, they came in a bewildering variety of stone or acid washes, slim, baggy, or boot cut, distressed, frayed, or slashed, and with a waistband that might hang anywhere between the waist and lower hips. It was difficult to tell whether people had dressed up for an occasion or simply come as they were.

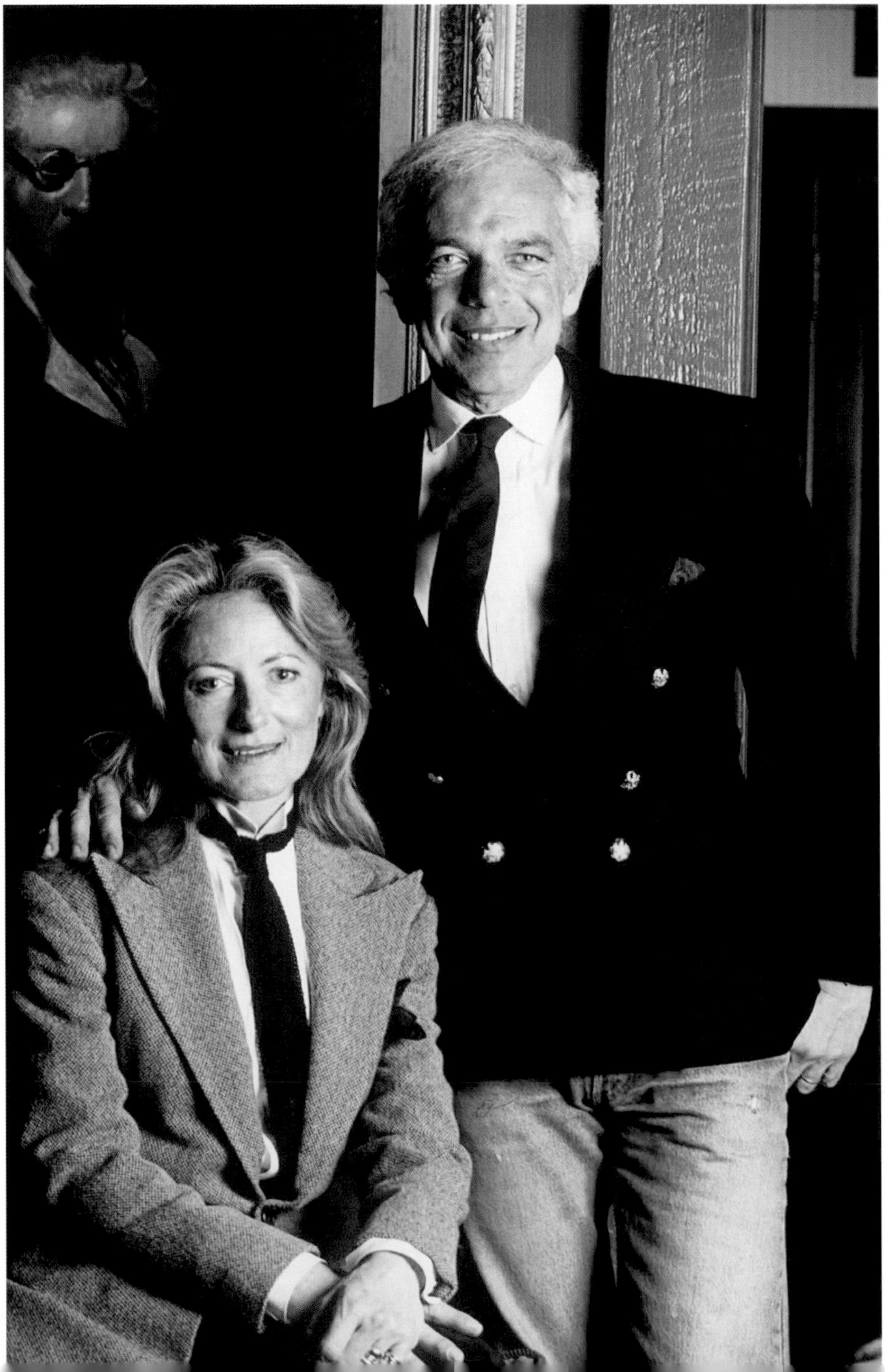

◄ Mr. and Mrs. Ralph Lauren in 1993, giving the seal of approval to the wearing of denim jeans as casual chic. The man-style tweed jacket, white shirt, and tie worn by Mrs. Lauren is an update on her husband's styling for Diane Keaton in the 1977 movie *Annie Hall.*

The Dot-Com Bubble

Around 1997, a huge number of new Internet-based businesses sprang up around the world. Known as "dot-coms" because of their Web addresses, they were mostly founded by young entrepreneurs and dealt in everything from last-minute travel reservations to pet insurance, trying to make the most of the new marketing medium.

At the same time, more adventurous individual speculation in the stock market and widely available venture capital created a lively and optimistic trading environment. Stock prices in the new ventures went sky high.

However, former Federal Reserve Board chairman Alan Greenspan's description of all this as "irrational exuberance" could have been regarded as a warning that it could not last. Many of the new businesses, either out of overenthusiasm or ignorance, abandoned standard business economics, hoping to increase their market share at the expense of the bottom line. The bursting of the dot-com bubble at the end of the decade, when thousands of companies crashed, marked the beginning of another recession in Western nations. Several companies, though, like Amazon and eBay, are still very much with us.

► Two outfits from the Spring/Summer 1994 collection by Ann Demeulemeester, both based on uneven, oversized layers and generous use of fabric. The suit on the left has an unstructured jacket and narrow but loose pants, matched with a billowing shirt. On the right, a long see-through tunic with ultra-long sleeves is worn over an asymmetric pleated top. Both suit and tunic show the designer's characteristic use of seaming and paneling on the outside of the garment.

▲ Dionne Warwick chose the casual, come-as-you-are look with distressed jeans for her appearance at a Los Angeles film premiere in 1998.

Deconstructing the Suit

The opening years of the decade saw the most obvious reaction to the eighties. The severely tailored eighties suit was literally taken apart by a group of young designers, headed by Martin Margiela, Ann Demeulemeester, and Helmut Lang. Looking back to Japanese design from the seventies and eighties, they produced looser garments with a distressed appearance—seams on the outside, uneven hemlines, preshrunk, wrinkled, and sometimes slashed fabric—which became generally known as deconstructivist. Usually in black but occasionally in other neutrals, the clothes often appeared to be inside out, oversized, or shrunken, but they were easy to wear and represented a welcome freedom from the restrictive power dressing of the previous years. They were also "serious" enough for the professional woman, and the style remained in vogue, with minor amendments, throughout the decade. Later nineties tailoring would be understated and soft, its simplicity concealing complex structure and masterful cutting.

► And the bride wore . . . white biker leathers over her sheath dress, in this early nineties outfit by American designer Norma Kamali.

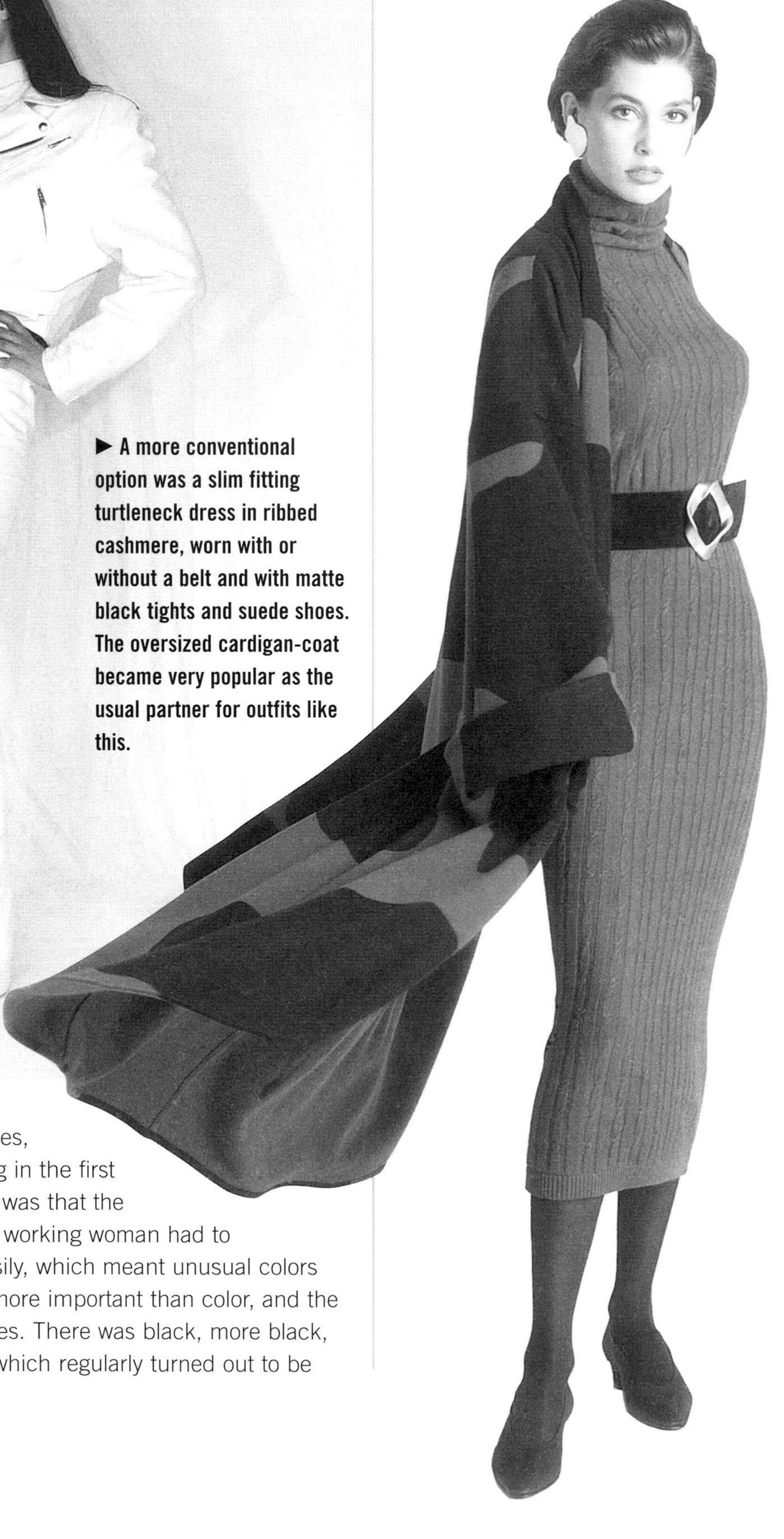

► A more conventional option was a slim fitting turtleneck dress in ribbed cashmere, worn with or without a belt and with matte black tights and suede shoes. The oversized cardigan-coat became very popular as the usual partner for outfits like this.

Color

After the garish, look-at-me hues of the eighties, color seemed to drain out of designer clothing in the first half of the nineties. A purely practical reason was that the increasingly popular capsule wardrobe of the working woman had to contain separate elements that combined easily, which meant unusual colors were out. In any case, fabric was becoming more important than color, and the new, softer tailoring looked better in flat shades. There was black, more black, and a continual search for "the new black," which regularly turned out to be

shades of gray or brown. Giorgio Armani and Donna Karan set the tone, working in a palette of neutrals: olive, khaki, taupes, and ecru, occasionally venturing into rust or dusty pink.

Mix and Match

As the decade went on, however, wearing a "total" look from one designer was out: the idea was now to put together an original outfit by mixing and matching from several sources. Women shoppers first created mix-and-match wardrobes from a single label and then, as the decade went on, confidently began matching items from different outlets. It was also chic to team one major fashion item with chain store accessories and flea market finds. It took effort, but the effect was all your own. This meant a big shift in the fashion industry. Design houses could no longer dictate, and fashion magazines found themselves hurrying to keep up with street fashion rather than previewing it.

As retro fashions came and went, they left odd elements behind them that were combined in a bewildering array. The aim seemed to be to put together the least compatible elements. Long jackets were worn over short skirts and skirts worn over pants. Contrasting, even clashing prints were paired in separates. For evening wear, leather motorcycle jackets were worn over glamorous dresses in silk or gauzy fabrics, frequently accessorized with a lot of costume jewelry and a fluffy feather boa. You didn't just break the rules—you stomped all over them.

▲ Biker chic was still in vogue at the end of the decade, as shown by actress-turned-model Sienna Guillory in 1999. Leather remained popular throughout the nineties, in increasingly softer textures and often matched with more conventionally feminine fabrics.

► Cross-dressing was one way of sharing the fashion experience among clubbers at the famous Kinky Gerlinky nightspot, where tinsel boas, fishnet, and leather were all part of the fun.

Boho Chic

Around the middle of the decade, the various retro revivals of sixties and seventies wear finally settled down into an eclectic bohemian look, later known as "boho chic." This featured loose, flowing tops, tunics over pants, fringed shawls, boots, or sandals according to the season, and lots of vintage jewelry or beads made from natural materials. Think late sixties flower child meets gypsy princess. It was soft, floaty, easy to wear, and very feminine. Style gurus picked up genuine vintage items from flea markets, while designers like Alberta Ferretti or Marni provided the professional version.

▼ Even supermodels like to find their own special clothes—Kate Moss hunts for bargains in a Paris street market.

◀ Sienna Miller, champion of the layered eclectic look, wears a shrunken jacket over a tunic over a dress with a fifties retro pattern. She's also carrying a pashmina (see page 40) to drape over the whole ensemble.

Heart of Darkness

A series of bloodthirsty civil conflicts occurred in the 1990s. Words like *genocide* and *ethnic cleansing* became part of daily speech as access to twenty-four-hour news coverage brought events into the home as never before.

The decade began with Saddam Hussein's invasion of Kuwait and the resulting Gulf War. Following his defeat, Saddam took revenge on the Kurds and Shia Muslims who had risen against him. The focus then switched to Africa. Some of the most appalling violence occurred in Rwanda, where an estimated 800,000 people were killed in just three months in an outbreak of ethnic conflict in 1994 between Tutsis and Hutus. It was reported that soldiers and police officers encouraged ordinary citizens to take part and that Hutu civilians were forced to murder their Tutsi neighbors. The Rwandan genocide shocked the world. Although 500 people were sentenced to death and another 100,000 imprisoned, many of the ringleaders evaded capture.

Another major trouble spot was the Balkans. The former Yugoslavia tore itself apart in an orgy of bloodletting, also based on ethnic and religious difference. Again neighbors turned on each other in revenge for ancient grievances. Servicemen and servicewomen from the United States, Britain, and other countries found themselves posted to war zones as arbitrators and peacekeepers in civil wars that they barely understood.

▲ The influence of Jean Paul Gaultier is clearly seen in this fantasy latex-and-leather outfit.

► Alexander McQueen's mold-breaking "bumster" pants won him a Dress of the Year award in 1996 and started the trend for daringly low-cut pants and skirts.

Flaunting It

But not every woman wanted to be a romantic peasant. This was still the era of the body beautiful, and many were intent on showing off as much of it as possible, especially when it was tanned and taut. Modesty was hardly in their fashion dictionary. British designer Alexander McQueen obliged with his "bumster" pants, cut so low on the hips as to reveal a bare midriff, underwear, and a lot more. Evening wear was sleek and slinky, with necklines slashed to the waist. It was often hard to see what kept these dresses on the body at all. Cher, famed for her stunning stage outfits, made a red-carpet splash with her Bob Mackie "headdress" outfit. And in 1994, Liz Hurley stole the show at the London premiere of the movie *Four Weddings and a Funeral* in a black Versace dress with plunging neckline and the sides held together by safety pins.

Free Nelson Mandela

On February 11, 1990, Nelson Mandela walked free from prison after twenty-seven years. He had been arrested as a prominent anti-apartheid activist and member of the African National Congress party (ANC), which the apartheid regime, and nations sympathetic to it, regarded as a terrorist organization. In fact, although armed struggle was an integral part of the ANC's overall campaign against apartheid, it had always been a last resort for Mandela, who remained steadfastly committed to nonviolence. On his release, Mandela worked closely with President De Klerk for a peaceful transition to a multiracial South Africa. Under his guidance, the ANC switched to a policy of reconciliation that facilitated that successful transition.

In 1994 the first free, fully representative elections were announced. The world watched as millions of black South Africans walked for miles and lined up all night outside polling places to cast their votes for the first time in their lives. To no one's surprise, Mandela was elected president.

The establishing of democracy in South Africa was greatly aided by the setting up of the Truth and Reconciliation Commission in 1995. Anybody who felt they had been a victim of violence could come forward and be heard, and perpetrators of violence could also give testimony and request amnesty from prosecution. The hearings made international news, and sessions were broadcast on national television. Later, they were to serve as a model for other countries faced with recovery from similar situations.

► **Liz Hurley and what became known as "That Dress." The barely-there Versace creation—which she maintained was a loan because she couldn't afford to buy one—was a marvel of engineering. It certainly helped her career, winning her a contract with top cosmetic house Estée Lauder.**

The Cult of Celebrity

Around the world, the public's obsession with the lives of celebrities knew no bounds. Pop stars, heiresses, sports personalities and their wives, Princess Diana—we just couldn't get enough of them. Reality TV, in the shape of *Big Brother* and *The Real World* and confessional chat shows hosted by Jerry Springer and Oprah Winfrey, fulfilled Andy Warhol's prediction of fifteen minutes of fame for the most ordinary people. MTV and a host of magazines like *Hello!* and *OK* showed us the inside of celebrities' homes, the state of their marriages, and, of course, what they

▲ **You hadn't really arrived on the celebrity scene until you were featured in *Hello!* magazine, although many later regretted having invited the photographers into their homes. Less than two years after this cover story, Lisa Marie had filed for divorce. As the appetite for gossip and sensational revelation grew, people's lives came to be regarded more and more as public property.**

wore, all in minute detail. The effect of all of this on the fashion scene was incalculable. New and often random trends were created overnight. Women flocked to their stylists for a hairstyle like Jennifer Aniston's character in *Friends* and raided stores for the Fendi purse carried by Madonna. Normally sensible golfers sent sales of khakis soaring, just because Tiger Woods wore them.

▼ **The boundary between reality and fiction was becoming blurred. To the many admirers of the TV sitcom *Friends*, actress Jennifer Aniston was inseparable from her character, Rachel Green. From 1994 on, each episode was carefully scrutinized for fashion tips as the apartment-sharing friends got to wear the latest girl-about-town fashions.**

▲ **The original ambitious blonde—Madonna in 1990 in the famous Jean Paul Gaultier outfit that spawned a thousand imitations. Other designers with a claim to having invented the long-running "underwear-as-outerwear" theme, with bras, basques, and corsets worn either alone or over other garments, were Versace, Dolce and Gabbana, and Vivienne Westwood.**

▼ More underwear-as-outerwear for material girls, in this leather-look outfit by Thierry Mugler. It shows the edginess of nineties fashion.

► Girl power rules—the message is loud and clear from Geri Halliwell of the Spice Girls at the Brit Awards, 1997.

Girl Power

The enormous success of artists like Madonna and newly created all-girl bands like the Spice Girls had everybody talking about "girl power." Confident and assertive young women were staying single, taking their careers into their own hands, and, most important, dressing to please themselves, not men. If they wanted to wear revealing outfits, that was their business. It all sounded great, but some expressed doubts as to whether young women were really more liberated or just pawns of the fashion-and-celebrity machine.

It's Great to Be Young

Youth was worshiped in the nineties. A lot of the clothes only looked good on young, super-slim girls, and the models seemed to get younger and thinner. After the bronzed, glamorous supermodel phase of the late eighties, the waif-like look of the sixties returned with a vengeance in the early nineties. This gave way to the tall, high-cheekboned, blond look as new models were discovered on the streets of the newly independent states of Eastern Europe.

The downside of this obsession with youth was that it made older women desperate to hang on to their assets. Alongside healthy organic eating and exercise, there was a massive increase in plastic surgery. Women barely into their twenties thought nothing of having eye tucks, tummy tucks, breast implants, and Botox injections to smooth out wrinkles.

Baby Chic

If it was great to be young, there was never a better time to be a baby. Offspring were suddenly in demand as the latest lifestyle accessory. In a curious throwback to the sixteenth century, children were often dressed like mini-versions of their parents. Infants in denim jeans and baseball caps gurgled in their strollers while ten-year-olds who just couldn't wait to be grown up were strutting their stuff in Lycra and crop tops in imitation of their girl-band heroines. While the market boomed, many parents expressed fears that the sexualizing of children at such an early age was unhealthy.

▼ Bicycling was heavily promoted as a healthy alternative to driving, although it took nerve to join the traffic.

▼ Dressing alike could be cute and harmless, but encouraging girls to dress in a style older than their years posed problems for many parents.

The World's Style Icon

The transformation of Princess Diana from shy teenager to fairy-tale royal bride to international fashion icon and probably the most famous woman in the world was astonishing. Throughout the decade she was rarely out of the headlines, whether for her charity work or the shock of her divorce from Prince Charles but mostly for her beautiful designer clothes and the elegance with which she wore them. She patronized emerging British designers and top foreign designers alike, being seen in the elegant simplicity of Catherine Walker day clothes and Victor Edelstein evening wear as well as jeans and baseball cap for taking her sons to school. In June 1997, just two months before her death in a car crash, seventy-nine of Diana's dresses were auctioned for charity by Christie's in New York. The sale earned over $3 million for her various charities, and the catalog alone, illustrating all the outfits, has proved to be a record of the fashion of two decades.

▼ Princess Diana wearing an embroidered white lace dress, one of the many designed for her by Catherine Walker, at a White House charity function in Washington in 1996.

Urban Sportswear . . .

After revisiting retro styles, the next style revolution took the most ordinary items of work wear, sportswear, and military clothing and served them up as fashion items. Garments usually associated with active outdoor sports like bicycling, mountain climbing, skiing, and snowboarding were given a new twist by adding fashion details or, in the couture world, by making them out of luxury fabrics. John Galliano produced fencing bodysuits in satin, while Karl Lagerfeld showed sequined surfing suits and silk puffer jackets.
Ready-to-wear collections included cargo pants, parkas, and hooded sweatshirts in silk and softly draping microfabrics, in pastel colors and metallic finishes.

► Louis Feraud, designer of this sleek silver hooded anorak, was just one of the couture names to take up the sportswear theme.

▲ **Were youngsters really fashion conscious or just following the herd? Cargo pants, in khaki or camouflage, and a sports-based T-shirt were the uniform of boys of all ages.**

▲ **Karl Lagerfeld's bizarre 1991 sequined surfer suit, definitely not designed to get wet.**

▲ **Top model Claudia Schiffer in couture camouflage at the 1994 Valentino autumn/winter show.**

...and Army Surplus

With half the world at war, it wasn't long before people were dressing like part-time soldiers. Multi-pocketed cargo pants seriously threatened jeans as casual wear. The genuine article was readily available in army surplus stores, but designer versions soon appeared. Pockets and epaulettes were featured on shirts and jackets, and camouflage prints in green and khaki or desert-issue sand were everywhere. Cartridge belts and purses shaped like ammunition cases made up the look. Although some felt that this trivialized war, it didn't prevent designers from taking up the theme. Critics debated whether making coveralls and army surplus

Fashion in Cyberspace

Computer technology revolutionized the fashion world. Most designers use computers at some stage in the design process, and laser printing on fabrics is widely used. But it was the Internet, born in 1992, that really changed the way we communicate, spend our money, and do business. By 1994, 3 million people were online: by 1998, this figure had increased to 100 million and was rising fast. Designs could now be sent from one country to another in seconds, which meant that chain-store versions of designer garments could be on sale within days of their appearance on the runway. In most cases this was legitimate, but infringement of design copyright by unscrupulous operators became a growing problem. Many of the major fashion shows could be watched on the Internet, and virtual fashion magazines were among the first in the field.

The Internet has also transformed the retail industry. Millions now shop online from all over the world, cutting out the chain stores altogether. And companies no longer need to gamble on which lines will prove to be best sellers. Benetton is just one company that no longer holds large quantities of stock but instead only makes as it sells, monitoring sales to ensure availability.

into luxury fashion was a stroke of genius or the biggest confidence trick ever. Either way, it proved to be the fashion revolution of the decade.

The Ethnic Look

The mixture of "exotic" styles became more and more eclectic. Indian, Chinese, and Japanese styles were very popular toward the end of the nineties. Chain stores sold imported silk embroidered jackets for evening wear, while the couture world saw more exotic versions, especially in the work of Jean Paul Gaultier. Rifat Ozbek, who is of Turkish origin and often uses embroidery and details from the Middle East, astounded the fashion world in 1990 with an African-inspired collection that included elements of Caribbean Rastafarian style.

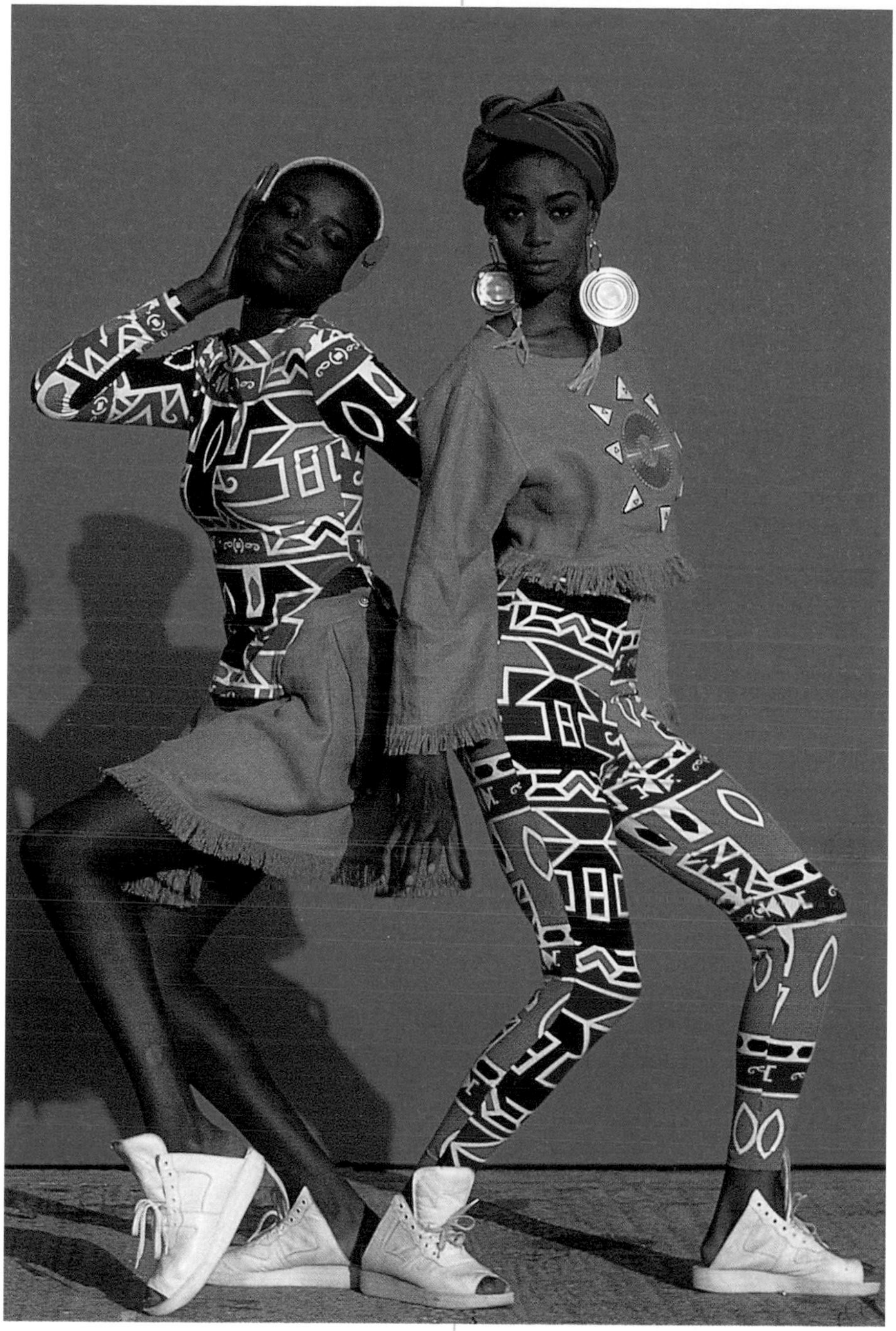

▲ African geometric-style motifs from Rifat Ozbek in his 1990 show.

► John Galliano went oriental in his 1997 show for Dior with this Chinese-style dress, modeled by Carla Bruni.

Showing Your True Colors

The ultimate fashion accessories in the nineties were body piercings and tattoos. Once the province of the punks, these fashions spread like wildfire. Studs and metal rings appeared in eyebrows, noses, lips, navels, and other, more intimate areas. Tattoos on women were popular, usually on shoulders and thighs, where they could be revealed discreetly. Those not brave enough to face the needle could have a temporary transfer tattoo or, following the Indian bridal tradition, a design worked in henna.

▲ There was no part of the body that couldn't be "improved" by the addition of some bits of metal.

Summing It Up

So by the end of this wayward, confused, and restless decade, who was wearing what? For color, glitter, and outright pizzazz—some would call it bad taste—a girl couldn't beat Versace, Gaultier, or La Croix. Teen fashionistas lined up outside the Prada store and came out looking like schoolgirls. Ladies who lunched went for the cool of DKNY, Oscar de la Renta, or Bill Blass, while those who worked for a living favored skirt or pant suits from Max Mara or Norma Kamali or the diffusion ranges of Armani and Jill Sander. Men felt comfortable in sport-based Tommy Hilfiger and Gap khakis or the reliably smart Ralph Lauren.

The young and streetwise wore—well, anything. In a fascinating article, American social anthropologist Ted Polhemus wrote in 1997 that young people tended to come together in "tribes," easily identifiable to each other by their clothing. This gave them a sense of belonging in a confusing world. He identified some of these as Goths, New Romantics, Psychobillies, Ragamuffins, Rastafarians, Ravers, Acid Jazzers, Grunge Girls, Cyber Punks . . . and many more. Which just about sums up the nineties: people made up the world to suit themselves.

◀ A real punk revival was difficult because the real things were out there on the streets, still maintaining that they were anti-fashion, while fashion houses fed back their style with a high price tag.

▲ Typically exuberant multicolored printed stretch pants and silk blouse by Gianni Versace for summer 1991. Versace's lively sixties-style color palette ensured that the company remained a style leader during the nineties.

► At the other end of the shade chart, Armani continued to lead the world in classic, comfortable, and easy-to-wear clothes for all ages in muted, quiet, neutral shades. Here, actress Claudia Cardinale dresses the part for a visit to the Armani store in London.

Millennium Fever

Approaching the end of a century inspired feelings that somehow time was running out. Governments rushed to complete the finishing touches on commemorative buildings and special events for December 1999—although some maintained that the new century should not begin until 2001. As deadlines loomed, a kind of panic set in. Religious sects awaited the end of the world. Rumors spread that the world's computers would crash on the dot of midnight on December 31, 1999: navigation systems would fail and planes would fall from the skies, stock markets would crash, and other apocalyptic horrors would follow. But in the end, none of this happened. In fact, the turning of the millennium was marked not by fire and brimstone but by the explosion of a million fireworks. As the message of the dawning of the new millennium spread across the datelines, nations attempted to outdo each other in increasingly impressive displays. And in the morning, the world got up and went about its business as usual . . .

Retro or Reinvention?

▲ Tie-dyed T-shirts came around again, but this time they were worn with irony: genuine hippie ideals didn't sit easily with the new materialism. An attempt to revive the Woodstock festival in 1994 met with dismal failure, and by the end of that year, the hippie revival was over.

Nostalgia Isn't What It Was

At the top of the retro nostalgia list were the sixties and seventies. In the early nineties, miniskirts, bell-bottoms, platform shoes, granny glasses, and bright jazzy prints from designers like Pucci appeared everywhere, often to the distress of those old enough to have worn them the first time around. Fluorescent colors from the early sixties—pink, green, yellow and orange—were a particular fad among the young, in socks, sweatshirts, shoelaces, and backpacks.

Tie-dye T-shirts were around by 1992, although no one dyed his or her own these days, and even denim overalls enjoyed a brief revival. Around 1996, the preppy or Mod look of the seventies was popular among teenage boys, closely associated with the Tommy Hilfiger line of smart, casual clothing.

Rebels With a Cause

Rei Kawabuko of Comme des Garçons led a punk revival in 1992 with her "Rebel" collection, in which wrapped and draped suits were decorated with PVC trim and models wore punk hairstyles. Amazingly, real punks were still around, now well into the third generation and looking pretty much the same as their grandparents. But in the face of so much trash and grunge culture from the professionals, they had lost much of their impact.

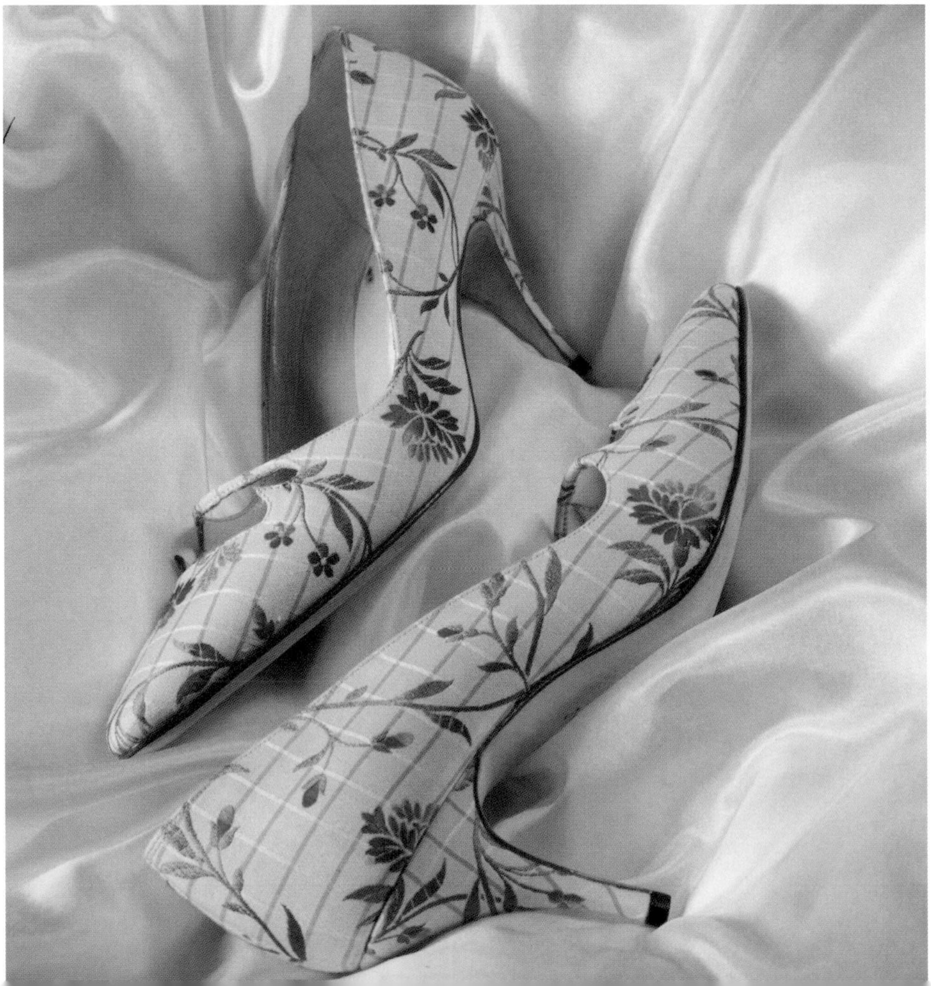

◀ Designers reinterpreted history in many ways. The design for these very nineties floral brocaded shoes by Manolo Blahnik (1996) was based on a carefully researched eighteenth-century fabric pattern.

Inspired by History

The past could also be used in a different way. Designer John Galliano's inspiration came from historical styles and even particular historical figures. His first show for Givenchy in 1995 reflected the whole history of twentieth-century fashion, recreating the style of each decade with his own contemporary twist. He has created pantsuits modeled on the style of Marlene Dietrich, draped evening dresses in the style of Mme Vionnet from the thirties, and devised collections based on Napoleon and the Russian imperial family. His cutting-edge technical skills and inventive use of fabric, however, mean that his work is far from simple pastiche. His fashion shows, usually staged in unexpected places, are real theatrical events.

▲ Another of John Galliano's forays into history produced this meditation on the period of King Henry VIII and Queen Elizabeth I of England. It combines the silhouette of male court dress with the kind of embroidery usually found on female gowns of the period and is set on a suitably androgynous figure. Little of this found its way into chain-store fashion.

► Another designer with an eye on history was Oscar de la Renta, who created this short redingote (frock-coat)-style coat in vivid, oversized plaid wool with fringed detail and jeweled buttons.

Expect the Unexpected

Karl Lagerfeld at Chanel summed up the philosophy of reinvention and unexpected combinations, especially when he updated one of fashion's timeless classics. He remade the Chanel jacket in glittery stretch tweed and teamed it with a frayed denim skirt, feather boa, and baseball cap. Other surprise offerings from the ever-inventive Lagerfeld included biker leathers over silk, fur overlaid with velvet, and embroidered leather.

▲ Karl Lagerfeld updates the almost-sacred Chanel suit for yet another generation.

◀ Stella McCartney's confident 1999 Chloé show featured floaty, girlie dresses paired with long boots, worn by Eva Herzigova, and lacy tops, seen on the model behind.

◄ **Hanae Mori has always been at the cutting edge of East-meets-West fashion. The nipped-in waist and unusual collar detail of this cotton suit from 1991 shows the continuing Japanese fascination with geometric design. Mori often paired cotton with wool and leather for textual interest.**

▲ **Ethnic embroidery motifs are strong in this 1997 jacket by Dries van Noten. Some of his embroidered clothes recalled the work of Elsa Schiaparelli in the thirties.**

Bohemian Rhapsody

From 1996 onward, bohemian romanticism emerged as the dominant female style. This could be said to be new, but it was still based on elements borrowed from the hippie and ethnic looks of earlier decades. Whether at street level or on the fashion runway, the look was layered. Dresses and tops in gauzy chiffon, slippery silks, and floral prints were worn under shrunken cardigans, coats, and shawls. Embroidery was everywhere, filtering down from the work of designers like Dries van Noten, who offered coats and jackets covered in ethnic stitchery. Velvet trim, ribbons, and beading made everything look more feminine than it had for a while. Designers to watch were the ever-romantic Galliano, Alberta Ferretti, and a little later Stella McCartney. Her collections of delicate, feminine garments blended frilly pastel silks and ribbons with slightly daring elements of tearing or discreet slashing.

New Kids on the Block

Ringing the Changes

To ride out the recession and capture the youth market, fashion houses had to reinvent themselves, which they did by making some radical appointments. It was all change at the top as a new generation took over. The former *enfants terribles* of fashion found themselves part of the establishment—and in the hot seats.

Lanvin, the oldest fashion house still in operation, appointed Claude Montana as top designer in 1990, but his designs were too bold for the traditional Lanvin customer, and he left after only two years. In 1995, however, Givenchy appointed the maverick John Galliano as its creative director, the first British designer ever to head up a major French couture house. When he moved on the following year to Dior, he was succeeded by fellow countryman Alexander McQueen, whose provocative designs and headline-grabbing shows had earned him the title "Bad Boy" of British fashion.

US designer Marc Jacobs, the former "Guru of Grunge," was appointed to develop the first ready-to-wear line at Louis Vuitton, while fellow American Michael Kors took over at Céline in 1997. In the same year, twenty-five-year-old Stella McCartney, daughter of former Beatle Paul, took over from veteran Karl Lagerfeld at Chloé, with less than two years' professional experience. Designers, like their models, were getting younger by the minute. And in their hands, street fashion and couture became virtually indistinguishable.

► The dramatic climax of Galliano's 1998 Dior show in Paris transformed the Palais Garnier into a fairy-tale palace.

▲ European fashion shows were no longer limited to traditional runways but increasingly took place in the most unexpected locations. For his 1996 London Fashion Week show, Alexander McQueen flooded a building usually used for flower shows and had models literally walking on water. Other unusual locations included a soccer stadium, a food market, and a bus station.

◄ As fashion events became more like site-specific performance art, designers became players in their own shows. John Galliano, seen here accepting his British Fashion Designer of the Year award in 1995, certainly lived up to the expectations created by his extravagantly presented shows.

Dior

Reinventing the Classics

Individual companies faced the same economic problems. Two examples were Burberry, rainwear manufacturers since 1856, and Scottish knitwear specialists Pringle, established in 1815. Their classic designs were associated with an older clientele, and the high quality their names guaranteed was no longer enough to achieve good sales. Both companies responded by inviting new designers to overhaul their trademark designs into more youth-oriented styles and by launching aggressive marketing campaigns.

In 1998, Kate Moss starred in Burberry's ads for new versions of the trench coat. This iconic coat was reborn in short lengths and unexpected fabrics like plastic and lamé. Pringle's traditional Argyle-pattern sweaters appeared in unexpected color combinations and variations of sleeve length and neckline, to be paired with T-shirts, jeans, and casual wear instead of pearls and tweeds. Ralph Lauren's classic polo shirts had a similar new lease on life: relaunched in brighter colors, they were suddenly cool again. Fashion was wiping out the age gap, as well as any remaining social distinctions.

▲ This shimmering purple dress and matching gray shawl with black velvet detail is typical of the work of Maria Grachvogel, who came to fame in 1994. Self-taught, she modeled her elegant satin and chiffon clothes on the sleek bias-cut dresses of the 1930s.

Will We Always Have Paris?

Since the 1920s, Paris alone had dictated fashion trends and decided what was "acceptable." By the 1990s, the fashion scene was being invaded by a new breed of innovative designers from all parts of the globe.

Britain offered the challenging work of Rifat Ozbek, John Galliano, and Alexander McQueen, as well as veteran shockers Vivienne Westwood and Zandra Rhodes. The Italian contingent was headed by the prolific Giorgio Armani, the innovative Franco Moschino, and the Dolce and Gabbana partnership, as well as the Missoni and Fendi teams. There was also a renewed interest in the House of Pucci, whose vividly patterned and colored sixties prints were very much back in vogue. From Sweden came half-French Marcel Marongui and from Belgium, Martin Margiela and Ann Demeulemeester.

◄ Vivienne Westwood showed no signs of toning down her provocative designs, although this little knitted mini, with matching gloves and hat, is a fairly restrained example of her nineties work.

► Stella McCartney shares the runway with two of her dresses at the 1998 Chloé show.

► This brilliantly colored scarf-print shirt by Pucci takes us right back to the heady days of the 1960s, perfectly matching the mood of the early nineties.

◄ The Burberry store in London's exclusive Knightsbridge district devoted a whole window to its advertising campaign starring Kate Moss.

◄ Martin Margiela is as understated as his clothes, refusing to put his name on any garment and branding them instead with a blank label. With visible stitching, exposed hems, tailor's markings, and external shoulder pads, his collections never fail to both shock and delight. This outfit is for Hermès, 1999.

America Makes the Running

Just Relax!

The general trend toward more relaxed everyday clothing meant that American designers came into their own in a way not seen since the forties. The "Big Three"—Calvin Klein, Ralph Lauren, and Donna Karan—could all be depended on to produce effortlessly chic, comfortable clothes with a sporty edge, the kind of thing that Americans have always done best. Calvin Klein in particular has acknowledged his debt to Claire McCardell, whose practical, versatile clothing laid the foundations of American classic casual wear in the forties and fifties.

Although they dominated the international market, none of the major brands could afford to rest on their laurels. Classics were continually tweaked to incorporate the latest trends. Ralph Lauren's trademark sporty Polo brand was joined in 1999 by RLX, a line of

▼ The popular American company Liz Claiborne maintained the theme of everyday sportswear in the early nineties with outfits like this reversible zipped bomber jacket and matching shorts, worn with a splash of solid color.

▲ Patriotic fashions abounded in the wake of the Gulf War. The American flag, always treated with respect, began to appear in a rather more relaxed context.

▲ At the all-American Tommy Hilfiger show in 1997, Kate Moss is treated to a rap performance by naughty-by-nature-boy Treach. The atmosphere of the show, the colors, and the sporty style all proclaim the essence of American cool.

▲ George and Barbara Bush set a new public tone for the nineties. For the inauguration ceremony, Mrs. Bush wore this chic outfit especially designed for the occasion by Scaasi, along with her signature fake pearls

active sportswear using new fabrics like Gore-Tex to keep pace with new, physically demanding sports like snowboarding. All three cleverly complemented their clothes with complete lifestyle collections of accessories and homewear, in which they were joined by the hugely influential Tommy Hilfiger brand.

White House Style

The inhabitants of the White House are a yardstick for American fashion watchers and as George Bush replaced Ronald Reagan as president, there was a distinct change of style. Whereas Mrs. Reagan had always worn the latest, most expensive high-fashion outfits and accessories, new first lady Barbara Bush favored a more relaxed, down-to-earth style that suited her age. Always correct but comfortably fashionable, her understated style spoke of "old money." Many of her outfits were created by America's foremost couture designer, Scaasi, whose worldwide standing increased considerably through this association.

◀ Another Scaasi design created for the older woman was this green silk ball gown with leg-of-mutton sleeves. Although it seemed that European couture was being taken over by a new generation of attention-seeking showmen, American design sold more quietly to real people.

Staying the Course

Nobody was better able to handle a sixties revival than Betsey Johnson, who made her name in that decade. She was part of the Andy Warhol set and dressed legendary models Twiggy and Verushka. Now in her fifties, she continued to produce colorful, sexy clothes, full of detail and decoration, which appealed both to the young and

Betsey Johnson, making a surprisingly late debut at London Fashion Week in 1998, proved that she could appeal happily to all age groups. Girls loved her Spanish Harlem chic (above), featuring a lilac floral cheerleader skirt worn over pedal pushers and matched with a cute bra top, while the accordion-pleated outfit on the right was elegant enough for any grown-up event. Johnson's work exemplifies the merging of American energy with European style.

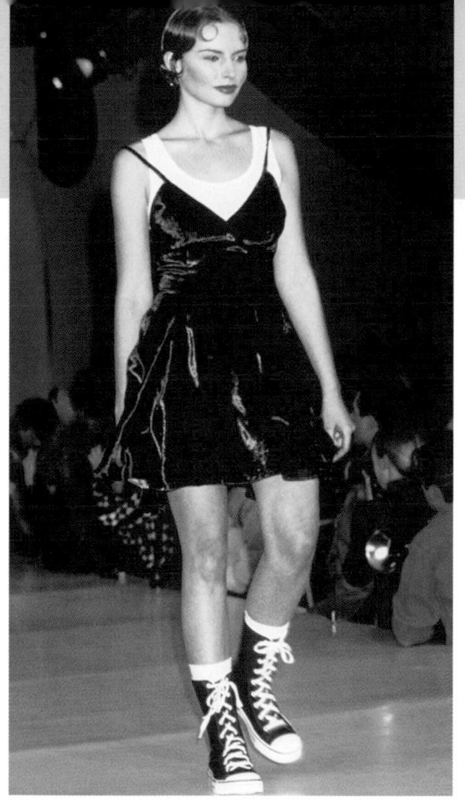

◀ **Norma Kamali is a true original, as shown by the name of her label OMO—it stands for "On My Own." Heir to the tradition of easy chic, she always has an eye on the sports field, and in 1994, she was showing short, flippy dresses, worn with or without body-hugging T-shirts underneath, and basketball boots.**

to their parents. Johnson's clothes are a celebration of sheer exuberance, ranging from screen-printed T-shirts and silver miniskirts to floral-patterned stretch tops and taffeta-and-lace embroidered dresses to suit every prom queen. Madonna, Cher, and Prince love her clothes, and in 1999, the CFDA (Council of Fashion Designers of America) created the Timeless Talent Award especially for her.

Wardrobe in a Bag

Another of America's pioneer designers who moved easily with the times was Norma Kamali. Back in the late seventies, she had been the first to introduce sweatshirt fabrics and was now working with clingy slip dresses, minis, sporty oversized T-shirts and pants, gym outfits, and sexy swimwear. Always cutting edge, in 1995 she launched a travel wardrobe of essential pieces, including pants, tops, and dresses in basic red, white, and black poly jersey. Easily washable and crease-free, a whole weekend's clothing could be rolled and packed into its very own "sack bag." The following year, Kamali presented her collection as a virtual reality experience on the Internet.

Rise and Fall

Isaac Mizrahi hit the fashion scene in the late eighties, hailed as the new, truly all-American designer. His clothes were big-city sophisticated, but characterized by simple glamour and nonchalant charm, modeled on the clothes of Norman Norrell, McCardell, and Halston. His early nineties collections took themes from American history, including Puritan-collared dresses and clothes inspired by Native American art. His 1994 collection was the subject of a popular documentary, *Unzipped*. Like John Galliano a little later, Mizrahi couldn't make a false step. Yet in 1998, following a funding crisis, he turned his back on fashion and went back to his first love, the theater. As well as continuing to design witty and exotic costumes for the dance companies of Twyla Tharp and Mark Morris, Mizrahi has written a cabaret show about his life, *LES MIZrahi*, and carved out a career as a TV personality. Flamboyant, openly gay, and happy to court controversy, Isaac Mizrahi lives at the point where fashion meets celebrity.

◀ **The bold statements Isaac Mizrahi made in the early nineties with these ethnic-influenced jackets, worn with miniskirts and zipped tops, showed just one side of his wide-ranging talent.**

Accessories Say It All

She's Gotta Have It!

As fashion became increasingly an eclectic mix of separate items, each individual element achieved an importance all its own. Shoes, purse, and scarves were no longer just color-coordinated backup to the main outfit: they were equally important component parts. In the second half of the nineties this gave rise to the "must-have" item, picked out almost at random by fashion magazines and promoted to the point of hysteria. There was panic buying, stores sold out in hours, and desperate shoppers joined waiting lists in the hope of obtaining the dream item. Those in the know ordered in advance as soon as the rumor of a new purse or shoe style began to circulate.

The Fendi Baguette Bag

This long, slim purse, so called because it recalled the shape of the French loaf, was the original "must-have" item. First launched in 1997, it reappeared in new patterns and fabrics each season so that devotees could add another to their collection. Limited-edition beaded versions are the most sought after, but almost any Fendi purse will fetch a high price on eBay. Madonna, Liz Hurley, and Sophia Loren have all been seen with one tucked casually under the arm.

▲ Purses were popular, especially glitzy ones like Liz Hurley's limited-edition Fendi baguette purse, studded with tiny mirror-glass disks. Another creator of highly original purses was British designer Lulu Guinness.

The Pashmina

This soft, warm, fringed shawl burst on the fashion scene around 1996. Pashminas are imported from Kashmir, in northern India, where they are hand woven from the softest hair combed from the underfleece of the central Asian mountain goat. The perfect emergency cover-up, worn with evening outfits and

▲ The pashmina looked good worn with anything and added instant chic to the most casual outfit. The lightness and crease resistance of this fashion staple is also demonstrated on page 40, where a woman is clutching a white pashmina in one hand along with her purse strap.

jeans alike, pashminas were initially available in a range of pastel shades, but toward the end of the decade, paisley patterned and beaded versions began to appear. Inevitably, cheap fakes soon flooded the market, but the pashmina remained a fashion staple well into the twenty-first century.

Fashion At Your Feet

If you were wearing shoes by Jimmy Choo or Manolo Blahnik, it didn't really matter what else you had on. Madonna once described shoes designed by Blahnik as "better than sex," adding that, "what's more, they last longer." Sarah Jessica Parker, Linda Evangelista, and China Chow all have Manolos named in their honor. Shoes came in all shapes, from the perilously high stiletto or "killer" heels—worn with pants as well as skirts and dresses—to the lower "kitten" heels, which took over at the end of the decade. Even styles based on beach flip-flops enjoyed fashion cachet for a while.

► The packaging is almost as elegant as the shoes themselves! Jimmy Choo's strict distribution system means that the collection is available only through upscale department stores and specialty boutiques in prime locations in New York, Beverly Hills, Las Vegas and London. A 1940s boudoir setting, with intimate style, velvets, and soft pastel decor, is the brand's trademark style.

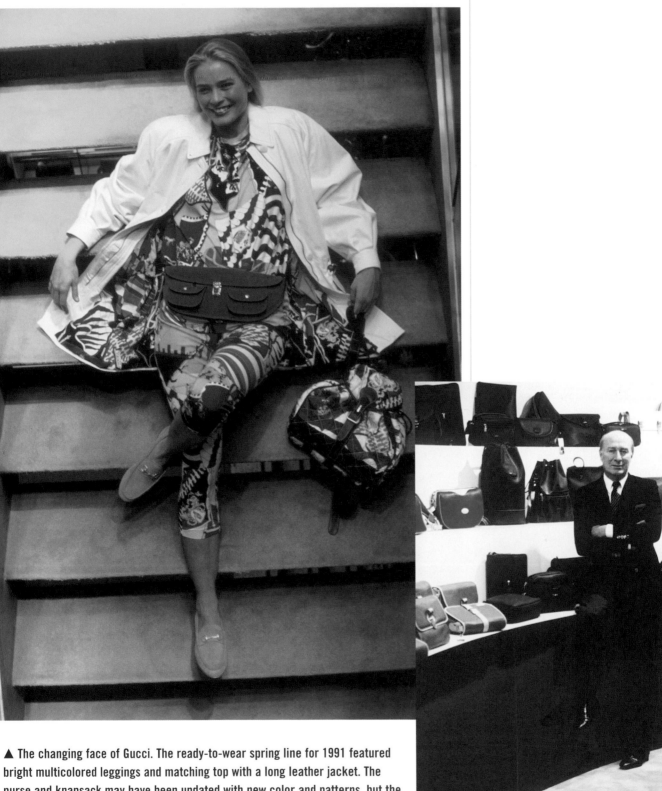

▲ The changing face of Gucci. The ready-to-wear spring line for 1991 featured bright multicolored leggings and matching top with a long leather jacket. The purse and knapsack may have been updated with new color and patterns, but the suede moccasins still carry the trademark horse-bit logo. Paolo Gucci is seen here *(inset)* with a selection of the high-quality bags and leather goods on which his company's fame originally rested.

▲ **The understated chic of the classic black nylon Prada purse is the perfect partner for any little black dress.**

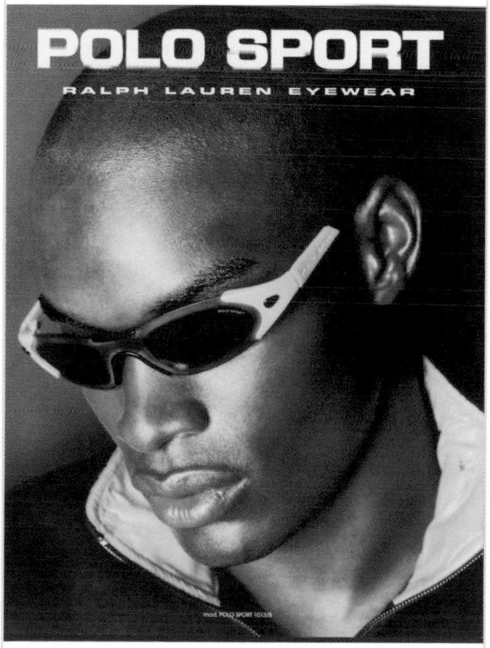

▲ **"Eyewear" was one of the fastest-growing areas of the accessory market. Virtually every design house marketed a range, concentrating especially on sunglasses.**

The Baggage Train

One of the remarkable features of the nineties was the rise of two Italian companies: Gucci, under American designer Tom Ford, and Prada, guided by Miuccia Prada. Both began as manufacturers of luxury leather goods and initially branched into clothing as an add-on to the accessories. By the second half of the nineties, both had grown into major fashion stables. Their success was due as much to brand-name recognition and dedicated marketing as to the quality of the clothes themselves.

Miuccia Prada launched her career in the mid-1980s with a single black nylon backpack, but her ready-to-wear collection four years later established her as a real trendsetter. The Prada look is cool and precise, yet always feminine, and the range of accessories in surprising prints and man-made fabrics allows fans to update their image season by season.

Although their stories are similar, Gucci and Prada are poles apart in style. Superstar designer Tom Ford's first collection for Gucci in 1995 was luxuriously sexy and had "jet set" stamped all over it. Overnight, this Old World accessory house became a mecca for the glitterati. Gucci loafers, whose traditional horse-bit logo is a reminder of the company's origins in saddlery, are about the trendiest casual shoes on the planet.

◀ **These elegant Manolo Blahnik boots from 1998 are made of plum-colored satin and feathers. Blahnik's status as a cultural phenomenon inseparable from celebrity was confirmed when Marge Simpson wore a pair of his mules during a 1991 episode of *The Simpsons*.**

The Word on the Streets

◄ Kurt Cobain of Nirvana, usually seen wearing baggy sweaters or layered shirts and vests, earned himself the title "King of Grunge." Cobain committed suicide in 1994.

The MTV Generation

The music scene, as always, was a major factor in street fashion. MTV, a cable TV network devoted to music videos and other material aimed at adolescents and young adults, was instrumental in spreading fashion news around the world. Shopping online and a rash of new style magazines like *Dazed & Confused*, *I.D.*, *Wallpaper,* and *Sleaze*, alongside the long-running *Face*, made it easy to keep up.

Grunge Style

The grunge look originated in Seattle youth culture and slipped into the mainstream via the music scene around 1991. It was particularly associated with bands like Nirvana and Pearl Jam. It was a unisex style, dominated by loose, layered clothes, stonewashed blue jeans, and plaid flannel shirts in dark colors like maroon, green, indigo, and brown, often worn over long underwear. Doc Martens-style shoes and boots completed the look. Originally an anti-fashion statement, grunge was soon made into a distinct fashion style when Anna Sui and, especially, Marc Jacobs took up the style and ran with it, followed by Dolce and Gabbana and Versace.

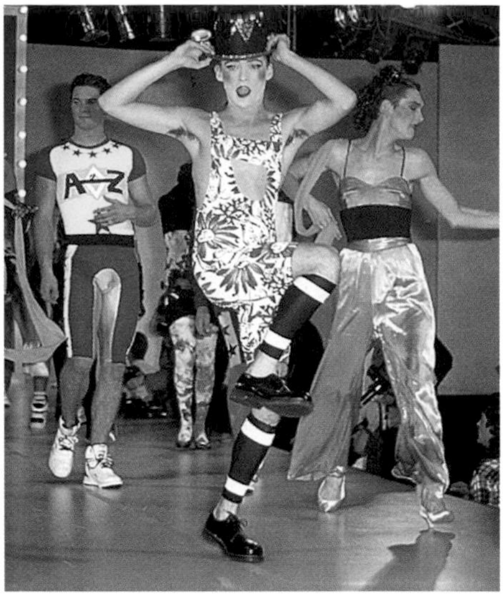

▲ Lycra exercise wear continued to influence club and street fashion. BodyMap, a design group much influenced by Vivienne Westwood and the Japanese avant garde, produced frequently outrageous collections throughout the late eighties and early nineties, but did not survive the decade.

▲ **British pop group Blur, seen here accepting a Brit music award in 1995, represented the Mod revival style of tousled hair and college-boy clothes.**

Britpop

While America was full of grunge and hip hop, Britain launched a 1960s revival led by bands like Blur, Oasis, and Radiohead. Often called Britpop, it was much influenced by the Mod scene of the late sixties, both in its music and its fashion. Bands wore clean-cut suits and Ben Sherman-style button-down shirts and generally looked neat, clean, and unthreatening. When this look got into movies, however, it was anything but that. Mod street fashions, long leather coats, and crisp suits were the order of the day in the slick, ironic thrillers of Quentin Tarantino and Guy Ritchie.

Spice Girl Power

If the Spice Girls didn't actually invent girl power, they certainly came to represent it. The group was designed to appeal to young girls, and their five distinctive personalities and fashion styles were promoted so that there was at least one Spice Girl that every girl could identify with. Their nicknames said it all.

▲ **The Spice Girls, each wearing her own typical kind of dress: (left to right) Sporty, Ginger, Baby, Scary, and Posh. The girls were being honored at the awards ceremony of the Prince's Trust, a charity set up by Prince Charles, in 1997.**

Victoria was named "Posh Spice" for her high-fashion Gucci dresses; Emma, in her little pink frocks, was "Baby Spice," Melanie B, who had attitude, was "Scary Spice," and Melanie C, usually seen in sneakers and sportswear, was obviously "Sporty Spice." Geri Halliwell's nickname was "Ginger" in Britain, but America called her "Sexy."

Hip-hop and Gangsta Rap

In the early nineties, pop rappers popularized the wearing of bright, neon-colored clothing and baseball caps. From the mid-decade, though, the more aggressive gangsta rap become the prevalent style, its overtones of crime and violence showing in fashion elements borrowed from street gangs and even prison inmates.

Generally, boys favored baggy jeans slung low around the waist, oversized sweatshirts with logos, undershirts under hooded sweaters ("hoodies"), boots or funky sneakers, and a bandanna tied around the head, sometimes with a baseball cap on top. "Attitude" summed up what it was all about. Style-leader Missy Elliot, queen of cool, made many of these previously male-only items acceptable for women, but for a more feminine look it was low-waisted skirts

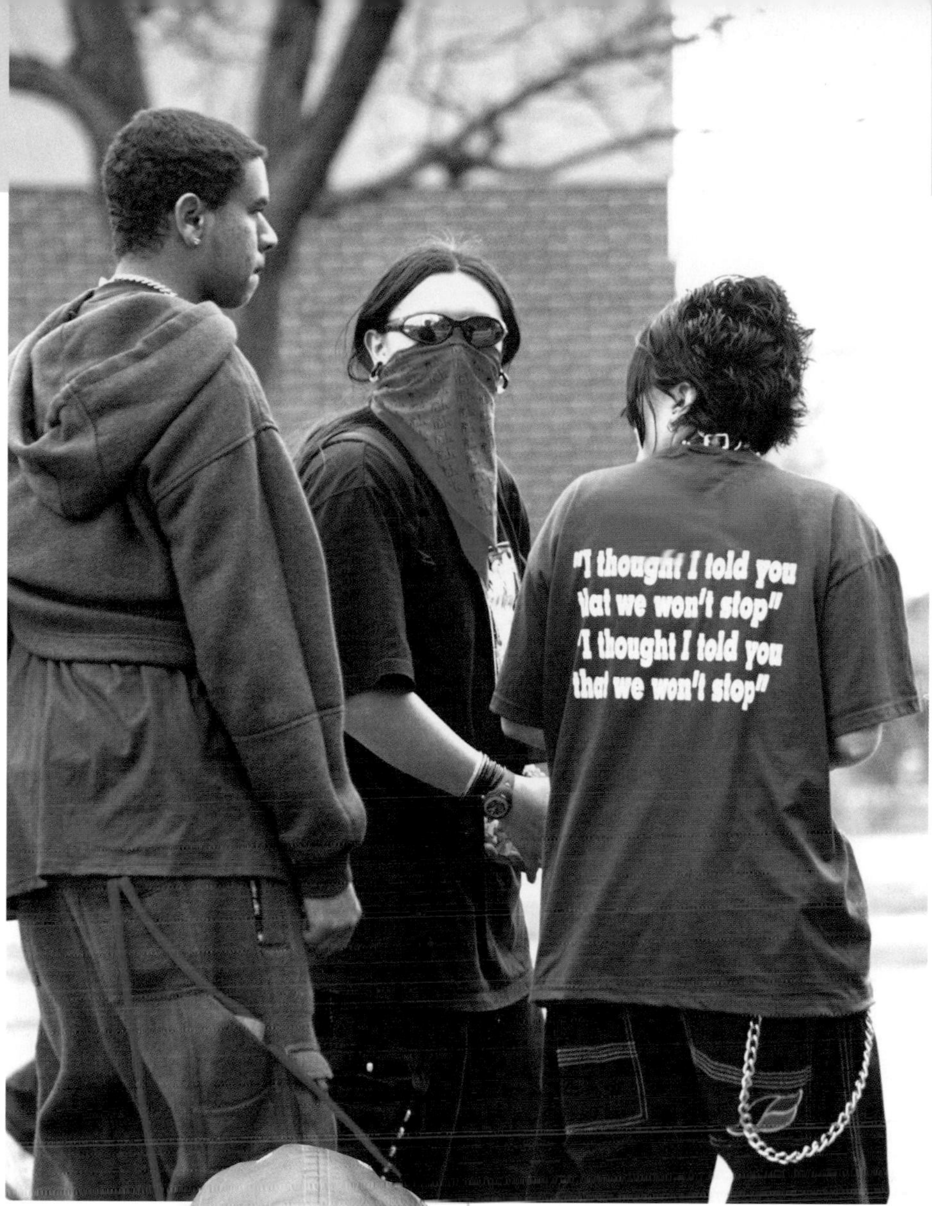

▲ Ice-T, actor, rock musician, and pioneer of gangsta rap.

◄ Young people at a music festival in the universal uniform of nineties youth. The boy on the left wears combat pants and layers of T-shirt and hoodie, while the one on the right opts for wide, baggy jeans cut as low in the crotch as possible and hung with punk-style chains and a slogan T shirt. Surprisingly, only one of this group is wearing sunglasses.

and jeans, tight tops to emphasize curves, and white fake furs. Designers like Gucci, Prada, and Versace were much in vogue for their irreverent, over-the-top glamour. There was a resurgence of traditional African-American hairstyles like cornrows and afros and, for both sexes, as much ostentatious jewelry as possible. Chains, watches, and rings in gold, silver, or platinum and preferably encrusted with sparkling precious stones were piled on. This became known as "bling" after the 1999 hit song "Bling Bling," but the term soon came to embrace the whole style and was often used in an ironic way by its detractors.

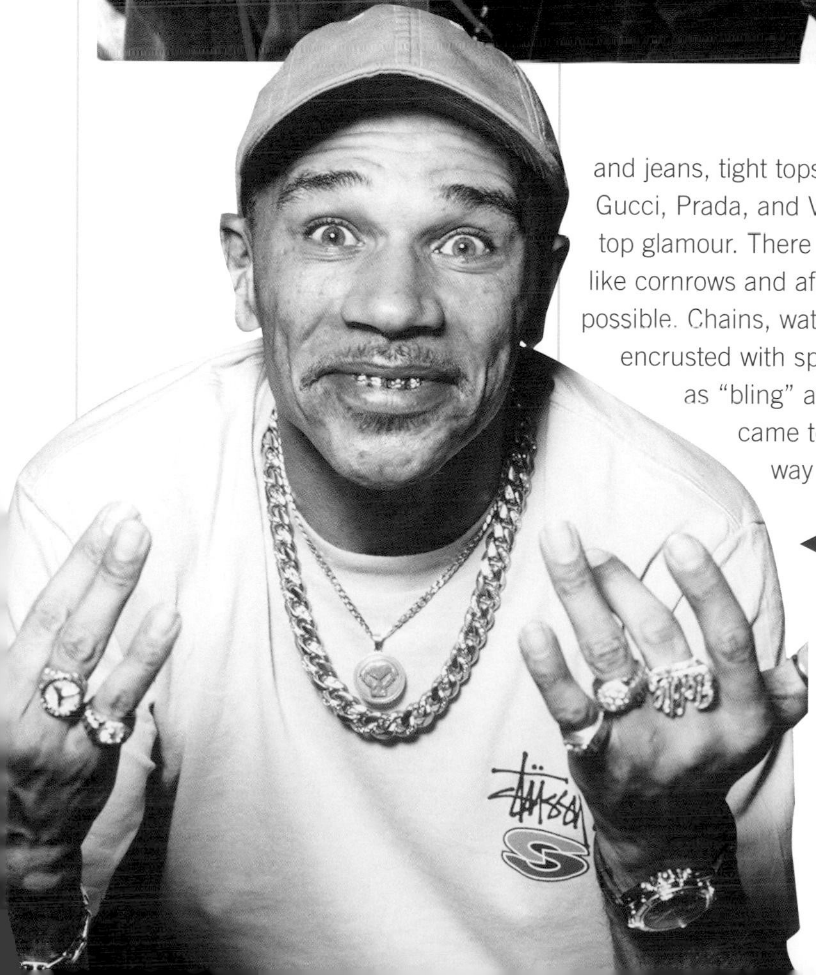

◄ DJ Goldie in 1997, wearing about as much jewelry as a man can pile on, including gold teeth. Note especially the Stussy T-shirt. Stussy originated in the surf scene of Southern California in 1980, creating customized boards and T-shirts. Within ten years, its classic military- and preppy-styled clothing had revolutionized the fashion world to the extent that in the late nineties, *Arena* magazine named Stussy the "granddaddy of streetwear."

New Man, New Market

Playing It Safe, In the Main

In the novelty-driven nineties, designers did their best to jazz up men's fashion with bright colors, patterned fabrics, jewelry, and even skirts. While some of the wilder ideas found their way into street fashion, most men over thirty just wanted minor variations on classic themes. However, more and more young men were prepared to admit an interest in fashion and their appearance. A new term, "metrosexual," appeared, coined by journalist Mark Simpson in 1994 and meaning "a young man with money and an interest in fashion who lives within easy reach of a city because that's where all the best shops, clubs, gyms, and hairdressers are."

Male Grooming

Once men accepted that it was okay for them to be interested in their image, they became the new target market of advertisers. The market in male cosmetics took off as young men, no longer content with aftershave and deodorant, began filling their bathrooms with face wash, exfoliants, hair conditioner, hand cream, cologne, and anti-aging products. Style icon David Beckham set weekly trends with each new hairstyle, wore nail polish, and freely admitted to borrowing his wife's underwear because it was more comfortable. The New Man had arrived.

▲ Men's toiletries, like their female counterparts, were sold on lifestyle promises. In a change from the open eroticism of many of the Calvin Klein ads, here sophisticated Nineties Man gets romantic with an elegant Christy Turlington.

◀ World soccer star and style leader David Beckham in 1998, with blonde highlights, a hint of designer stubble, and one of his wife's sarongs. Beckham's sensitive good looks, coupled with his athletic ability, made him the epitome of the nineties New Man. His marriage to Spice Girl Victoria Adams (Posh) confirmed them as one of the media world's top celebrity couples.

▲ Tommy Hilfiger swept into London Fashion Week in 1996 with his typical cool take on the almost-a-suit trend, showing coordinating checked blazers worn with cotton pants of different leg width and a hint of golfing shoe.

▲ Liam Gallagher of Oasis and his wife, Patsy Kensit, illustrate the bewildering variety of ways one could "dress" for the occasion. While she wears an elegant evening dress for this 1999 red-carpet film premiere, Gallagher sports a buttoned-up parka and jeans. It seemed that nothing was considered inappropriate.

Dressing for the Occasion

For the older man, the welcome appearance of Friday wear and urban sportswear meant that tried-and-true items like polo shirts, sweaters, and khakis became staple items. Ralph Lauren, Tommy Hilfiger, and Donna Karan were always on hand to supply a new slant on the kind of smart casuals they had always done best. But when the novelty wore off, men began to long once more for something formal, for a sense of occasion.

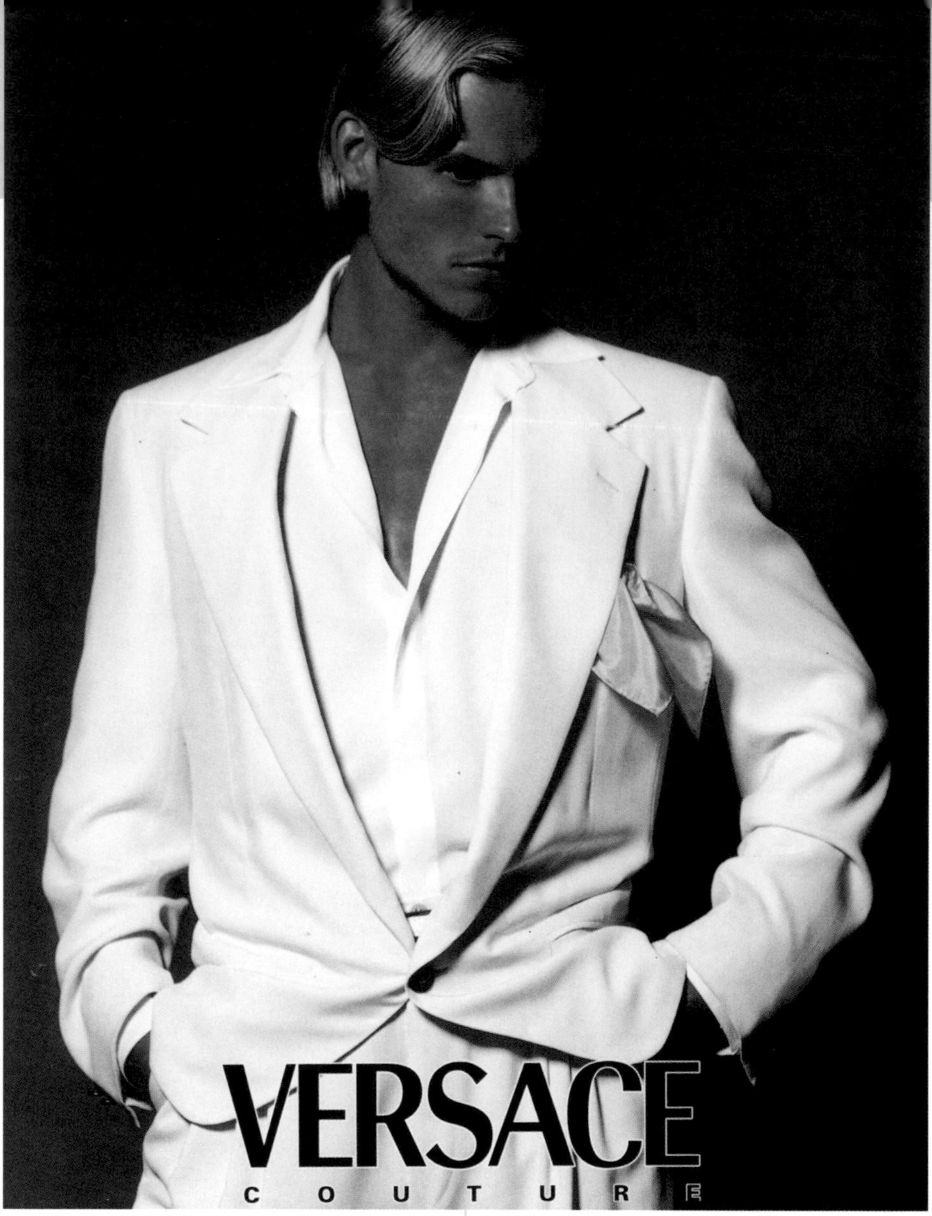

Retro Style, New Fabric

Men's tailoring saw a return to the classic look of the sixties, updated through soft construction and luxury fabrics. At the beginning of the nineties, formal wear for men and women had favored unstructured, slightly oversized suits and jackets. This gave way to sharper tailoring and a concentration on feel-good fabrics like mohair, alpaca, and lightweight woolen blends. Suzy Menkes's headline in the *International Herald Tribune* for January 1996 summed it up: "Cut, Color and Class." Impeccable tailoring and new stretchy fabric blends meant that clothes remained comfortable while following the body more closely. Suits had the elegant look of classic British tailoring: a slimmer line, single- or double-breasted jackets with narrower shoulders, subtle shaping, side vents and slight flare at the waist, and trousers with no pleats or cuffs. Colored shirts by Thomas Pink or Turnbull & Asser, now well established in New York, completed the British look.

▲ This ad for Versace male couture simply shouts "casual chic!"

Arty Chic

A universal trend, adopted particularly by men in the art and movie worlds, was to wear a T-shirt or three-button polo instead of a shirt and tie under a suit or jacket by Armani, Hugo Boss, or Paul Smith. This was the height of minimalist chic. More challenging, and probably best left to the young and fit, were Helmut Lang's ultra-minimal narrow trousers, three-button jackets, and clingy T-shirts in high-tech fabrics.

Super-tailoring

Ready-to-wear suits from the major labels were of good quality, but there was also a growing market for hand-tailored suits. Those who could afford that extra touch of class flocked to London, where Ozwald Boateng and Timothy Everest

► Movie star Jeremy Northam illustrates the prevailing look for the late nineties: slim-cut gray suit with dropped-waistline pants and a silky V-necked T-shirt.

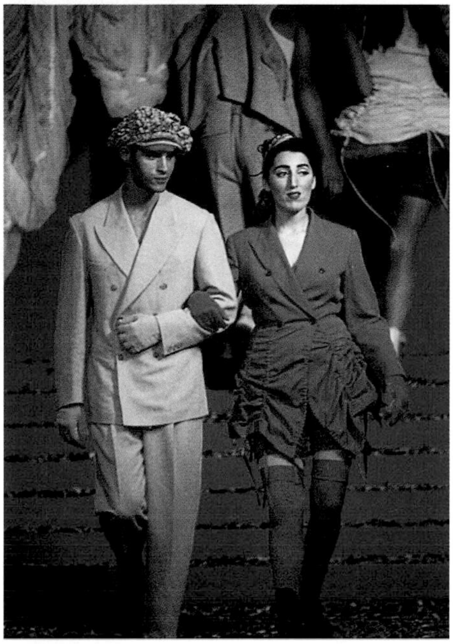

▲ Setting one of maverick Jean Paul Gaultier's designs from the early nineties alongside these later outfits confirms that on the whole, men just want to look good in a fairly traditional way. None of these radical attempts to get men into bright colors, odd headgear, skirts, or sarongs ever really caught on. In the end, it seems, men just refuse to be fashion victims.

► Ozwald Boateng, impeccably turned out for the 1996 Premier Menswear Exhibition. Boateng transformed the world of men's tailoring through his attention to detail and intelligent use of modern fabrics. Although it isn't clear from this example, the formality of the modern tailored suit was often undercut by the subversive use of a bright or patterned silk lining.

were causing a revolution in the conservative world of Savile Row. Boateng's style tip was for trousers without cuffs, a colored shirt (as long as it matched the tie), a silk handkerchief in the pocket, cuff links, and a touch of shirt showing under the sleeve. It was like a return to the formality of the thirties.

Fashion Technology

Rainwear from the Kitchen

New fabrics were flooding onto the market. In 1991, DuPont found a new use for the Teflon protective finish previously used on pots and pans. Teflon's excellent water and stain-repelling qualities made it perfect for use on outdoor wear. But there was much more to come.

▲ Rifat Ozbek was just one of the designers who experimented with vinyl in the early nineties. The fabric was usually associated with club wear and a kind of glam-rock revival. It also made frequent appearances in the underwear-as-outerwear period, enjoyed for its erotic overtones.

▲ When students at St. Martins College were asked to experiment with natural and organic forms to produce designs for the new millennium, some of the results were wildly imaginative.

Marvelous Microfibers

Whereas the wonder fabrics of the previous decade, like Lycra, had concentrated on cling and fit, research now had more to do with improving drape and flow. Man-made microfibers are ultra-fine—twice as fine as silk, three times finer than cotton, and six times finer than wool. Their high thread density means they have a greater number of air chambers and tiny pores, allowing the skin to breathe and the body to regulate temperature more easily. They also provide reliable protection against wind and rain, all qualities that make them perfect for active sportswear. In the fashion world, microfiber garments have a graceful flow and a silk-like feel and are extremely comfortable.

Tencel

One of the most important developments in this area was Tencel, a fiber made from the natural cellulose found in wood pulp. Similar to rayon in feel, it is soft, breathable, lightweight, quick drying, and comfortable. It's also shrink-resistant, durable, and easy to care for and, because of the fibers' high absorbency, can be dyed easily. Blended with other fabrics, Tencel enhances their inherent properties, introducing new softness and drape to wool and improving the shape retention of stretch fabrics, while blended with cotton and linen, it increases suppleness and luster.

Working Wonders

Miuccia Prada was particularly significant in the use of new fabrics. Exploiting nylon, mesh, and the new fabrics intended for extreme weather sports like bicycling, skiing, and climbing, she created an entirely new way of dressing.

► The unmistakable style of Prada, shown in Milan Fashion Week, 1998—no-frills tailoring and man-made fabrics expertly cut.

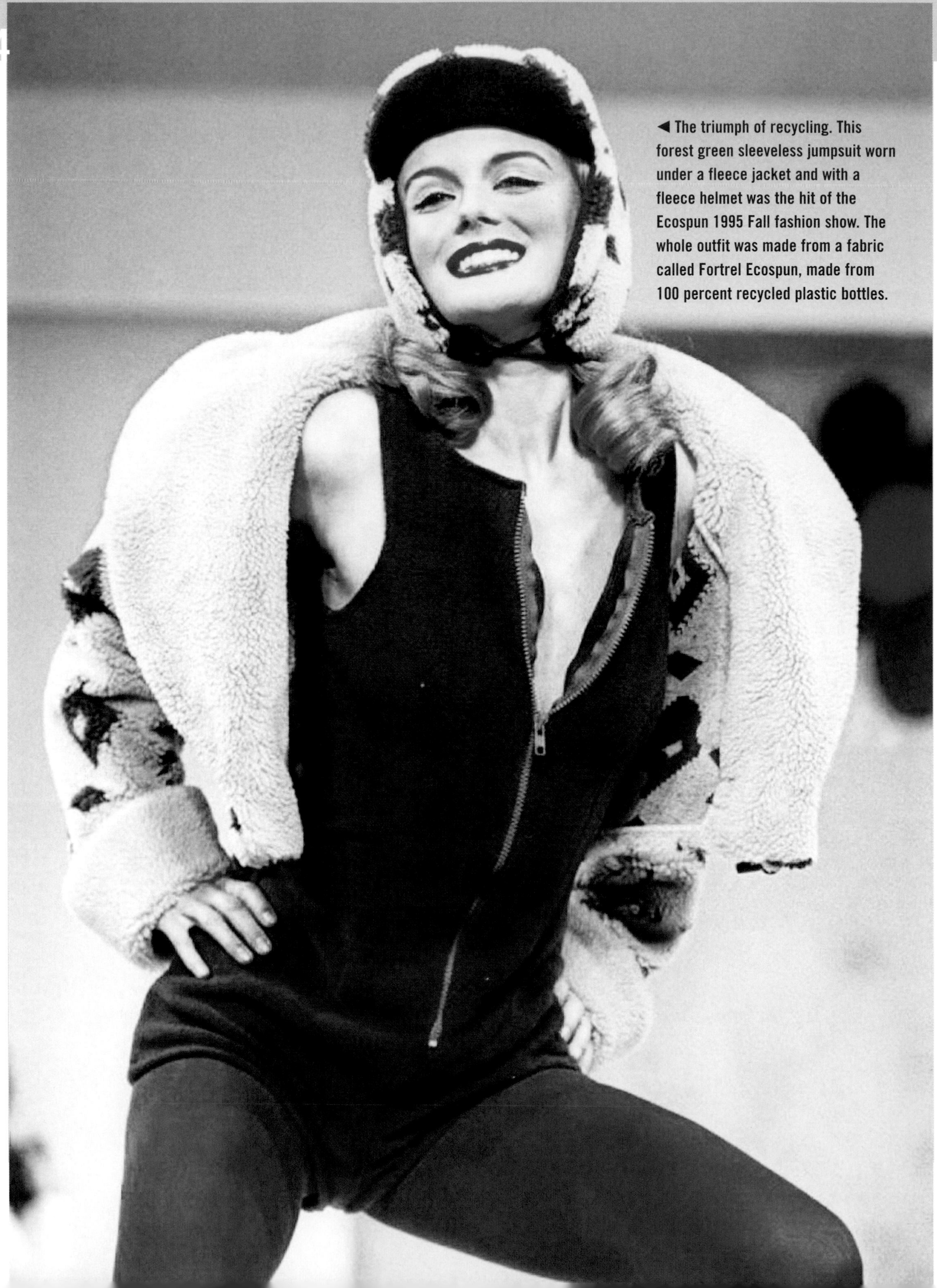

◄ The triumph of recycling. This forest green sleeveless jumpsuit worn under a fleece jacket and with a fleece helmet was the hit of the Ecospun 1995 Fall fashion show. The whole outfit was made from a fabric called Fortrel Ecospun, made from 100 percent recycled plastic bottles.

▲ **Hussein Chalayan's approach to fashion is almost that of a scientist. This woman's jacket, from a 1995 ensemble, is created entirely from photographically printed paper, which gives its floral decoration an extraordinarily delicate quality.**

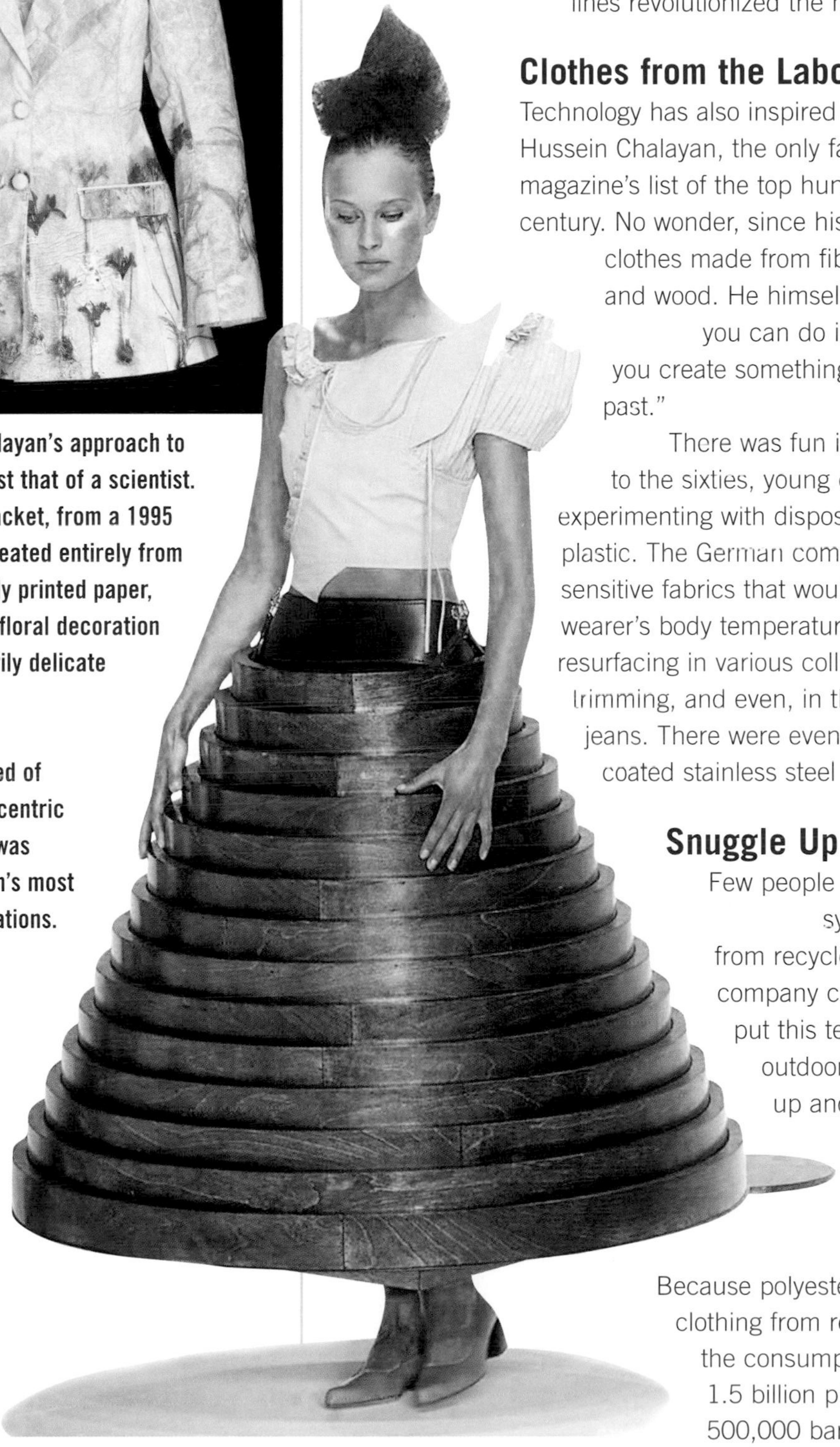

► **A skirt formed of collapsible concentric wooden hoops was one of Chalayan's most celebrated creations.**

Another cutting-edge experimenter was Helmut Lang, known for minimal garments that depended on perfect fit. Lang shot to fame in 1994 when his "Trash and Elegance" collection included a dress made of fused rubber and lace. His use of microfibers in his urban sportswear and couture work wear lines revolutionized the mid-nineties.

Clothes from the Laboratory

Technology has also inspired avant-garde designers like Hussein Chalayan, the only fashion designer to feature in *Time* magazine's list of the top hundred innovators of the twentieth century. No wonder, since his collections have included clothes made from fiberglass, paper, sculpted metal, and wood. He himself has stated, "The only new work you can do in fashion is via technology. It lets you create something you couldn't have done in the past."

There was fun in the 1990s, too. In a throwback to the sixties, young designers were again experimenting with disposable dresses made of paper and plastic. The German company Merck developed heat-sensitive fabrics that would change color according to the wearer's body temperature. PVC, the sixties favorite, kept resurfacing in various collections as jackets, rainwear, trimming, and even, in the work of Rifat Ozbek, as stretch jeans. There were even clothes made from polyester-coated stainless steel and aluminum yarn.

Snuggle Up with a Soda Bottle

Few people realized that their soft, cozy, synthetic fleece jacket was made from recycled plastic bottles. In 1993 a company called Patagonia was the first to put this technology into use for its range of outdoor wear. The bottles were chopped up and melted, then drawn out into long strands, which were spun and woven. Each garment used around twenty-five one-gallon drink bottles. Because polyester is petroleum based, making clothing from recycled polyester cuts down on the consumption of raw materials. Recycling 1.5 billion plastic bottles saves around 500,000 barrels of oil a year.

Fashion with a Conscience

The Fur Debate

At the beginning of the decade, the anti-fur lobby seemed to be gaining ground. Organizations like Lynx and PETA (People for the Ethical Treatment of Animals) campaigned against the use of fur, supported by celebrities from the film and fashion world, including Sir Paul McCartney and his designer daughter Stella, Charlize Theron, and Ellen DeGeneres.

One of the most famous campaigns was the 1997 PETA poster that said: "I'd Rather Go Naked Than Wear Fur" and featured five supermodels—Naomi Campbell, Christy Turlington, Claudia Schiffer, Cindy Crawford, and Elle Macpherson—doing just that. Madonna, too, wore a T-shirt declaring: "Fur is Worn by Beautiful Animals and Ugly People." Calvin Klein announced that he would no longer use fur in his collections, and others followed suit, using faux fur for trims and whole garments.

However, just months later Naomi Campbell was seen modeling a fur coat in the Milan show, and by the end of the decade, fur was back in fashion. Dolce & Gabbana, Fendi, Marc Jacobs, John Galliano, and Alexander McQueen all made the most of the world's most controversial "fabric."

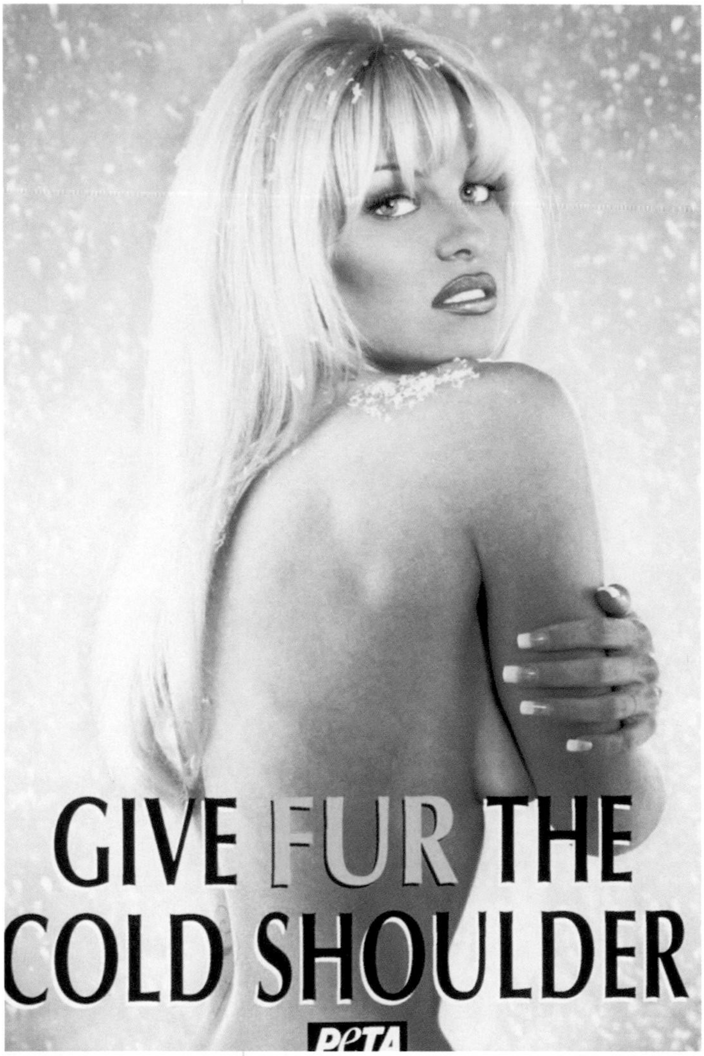
GIVE FUR THE
COLD SHOULDER

▲ Pamela Anderson was one of many stars who used her celebrity profile to promote the anti-fur and anti-cruelty campaigns. The posters were given added intellectual weight by their cleverly worded slogans.

◄ Fake furs and animal-print fabrics enjoyed wide popularity. They offered the traditional luxury, warmth, and softness of animal skins without the cruelty, although many who opposed the fur trade questioned why anyone would want to wear even a fake dead creature.

► New Man was eco-aware, took his turn at child care and advertised the fact that he bought his clothing from the catalog of the pioneering organization Greenpeace. Although there was still a long way to go, such attitudes marked a change in the general consciousness as concern about the world's resources and the increase in global warming became more urgent.

Back to Nature

Romeo Gigli's 1991 collection featured tree bark fabrics. Although clearly impractical in retail terms, these were instrumental in setting off a trend for rough-weave fabrics in natural colors of ecru and stone. Even this was not without its problems, however, since the dyeing process used on many of the "natural" fabrics made them less environmentally friendly than they appeared. British designer Katherine Hamnett has always been at the forefront of environmental concern. She has supported the use of "green cotton," produced without the use of pesticides on special plantations. Her "green" T-shirts remain best sellers.

Putting Smoking Out of Fashion

In 1998, top models and designers called on the fashion industry to stop using cigarettes as props in fashion photography. They were concerned that making smoking look cool and glamorous encouraged young people to smoke and was damaging their health. To launch the "Put Smoking Out of Fashion" campaign, Jacques Azagury, who designed clothes for Princess Diana, produced an exclusive dress that was signed by more than forty top fashion personalities, including supermodel Christy Turlington and designers Issey Miyake and Sonja Nuttall. The dress was put on display at the famous Central Saint Martins College of Art and Design in London, whose graduates include John Galliano and Alexander McQueen.

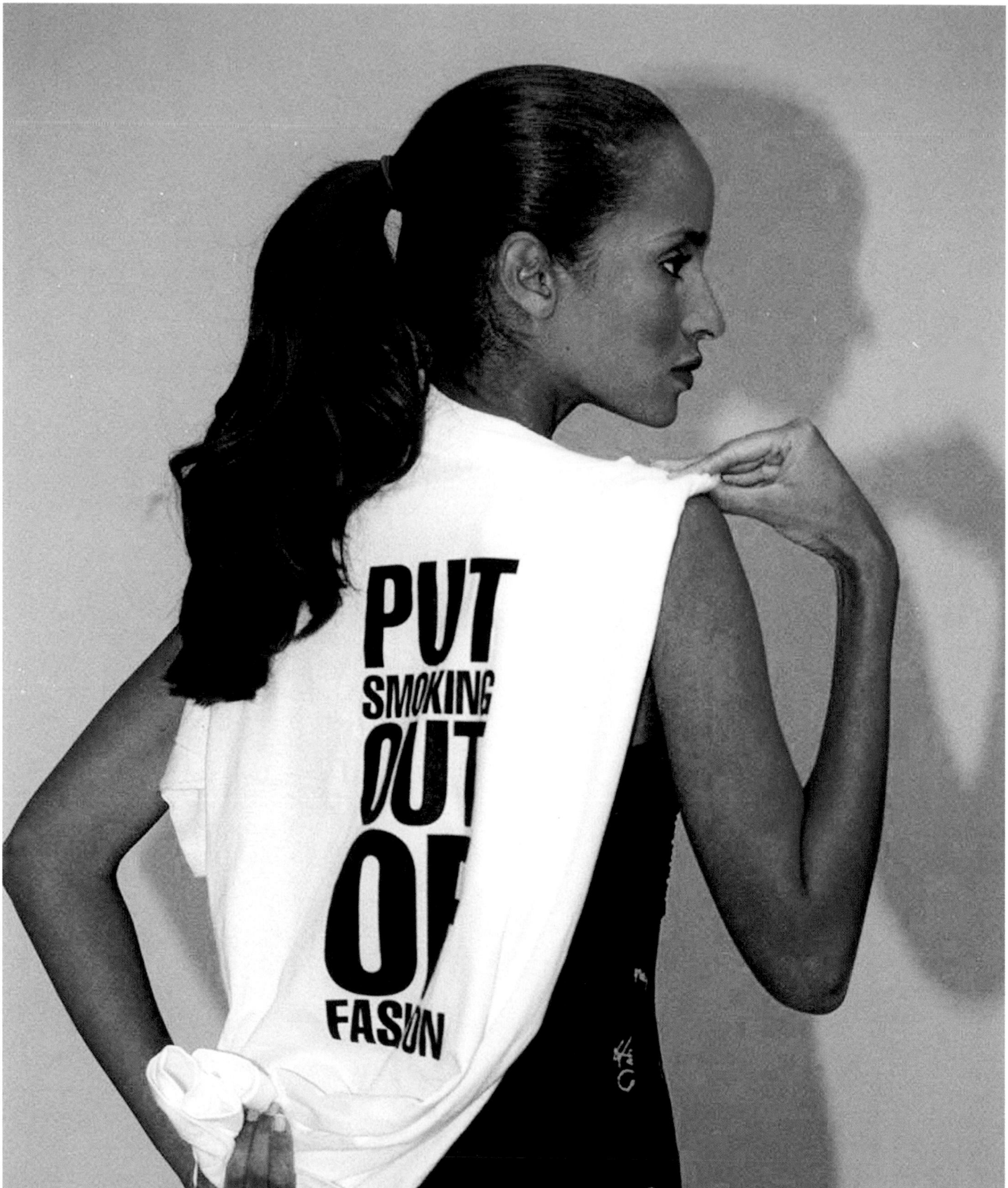
PUT
SMOKING
OUT

◄ The "Put Smoking Out of Fashion" dress, signed by luminaries of the fashion world, and the T-shirt that helped promote the campaign. Smoking among young people was a growing cause for concern during the nineties, still on the increase despite the fact that the link with lung cancer was widely acknowledged.

► Under her three-quarter-length coat and cropped trousers, Aimée Mullins shows off her ultra-fashionable, and very personal, "boots." Viewers at the fashion show were at first taken in and believed that she was, in fact, wearing wooden boots—particularly since the designer was Alexander McQueen, from whom people had come to expect the unexpected.

Striding Out in Style

Among the extravagant theatricals of fashion shows, there were inspiring moments. Aimée Mullins, already known as a Paralympic athlete, made her debut as a fashion model in Alexander McQueen's 1999 summer show. She was dressed in a tight bodice and what looked like hand-carved wooden boots but were, in fact, artificial legs. Aimée Mullins, who had had both legs amputated at the knee as a baby, stole the show and went on to launch a career as an actor.

Make It Cheap, Sell It Dear

As the clothing market became more competitive, companies switched their manufacturing to the developing world, where workers were paid very low wages to produce garments that then sold at top prices. There was an outcry about exploitation. After an international campaign of media criticism and consumer pressure, in 1995 Gap was the first major North American retailer to accept independent monitoring of the working conditions in a contract factory producing its garments. Many followed suit, but the doubts remained.

There was a question, too, about where fashion would be heading in the next decade. It looked as if the nineties had seen revivals of every possible style, every novelty of fabric and cut. The rule book had been torn up and thrown away—fashion was now what anyone said it was. After such radical upheaval, only a brave commentator would try to predict the direction of fashion in the new century.

Chronology

News

1990 Reunification of Germany.
Boris Yeltsin elected president of Republic of Russia.
Iraqi invasion of Kuwait initiates first Gulf War.
Nelson Mandela released from jail after twenty-seven years.

1991 USSR is dissolved and renamed Commonwealth of Independent States (CIS).
Civil war in Yugoslavia.
Famine in Sudan.
Military junta takes power in Thailand.
Burmese leader Aung Sang Suu Kyi awarded Nobel Peace Prize.

1992 Civil war in Algeria brings Islamic parties into local government.
Bill Clinton elected President of the United States.

1993 Czechoslovakia splits into Czech and Slovak republics.
Israel's Yitzhak Rabin and Palestinian Yasser Arafat sign peace accord.

1994 Russians invade breakaway region of Chechnya.
Civil war in Rwanda: thousands die in genocide.
North Korea's Kim Il Sung dies.

1995 End of fighting in Bosnia.
Yitzhak Rabin assassinated by Jewish extremist.
Nigeria executes environmental campaigners, including Ken Saro-Wiwa.

1996 Benjamin Netanyahu elected prime minister of Israel.
Russia and Chechnya sign peace treaty.
United States bombs southern Iraq.
Taliban seize Kabul, Afghanistan.

1997 Diana, Princess of Wales, killed in car crash.
Uprising in Albania: government falls.
Tony Blair becomes British prime minister.
Death of China's Deng Xiaoping.
Britain returns Hong Kong to China.

1999 Good Friday Accord promises peace in Northern Ireland.
Civil war in Kosovo.
India and Pakistan conduct atomic tests.
President Clinton impeached over Monica Lewinsky affair.

1999 Northern Ireland becomes self-governing.
Nelson Mandela retires and is succeeded by Thabo Mbeki.
Boris Yeltsin resigns and is succeeded by Vladimir Putin.
Military coup in Pakistan.

Events	Fashion
Hubble Space Telescope launched. Margaret Thatcher resigns as British prime minister.	R. Ozbek shows all-white collection. Philip Treacey opens own millinery business. Halston dies. Anna Sui has first fashion show. Madonna popularizes Dolce & Gabbana's rhinestone bodice. Valentino exhibition in Milan.
Cyclone in Bangladesh kills 125,000 people.	Tencel first made. Prada launches Miu Miu diffusion line. Ann Demeulemeester opens own Paris showroom. Dolce & Gabbana's Parfum launched and wins Accademia del Profumo award.
Riots in Los Angeles after white policemen beat up black motorist.	Alexander McQueen opens own fashion business in London. Vivienne Westwood's platform shoes trip up Naomi Campbell. Patrick Cox designs "Wannabe" loafers. Issey Miyake launches Pleats Please ready-to-wear. Madame Grès, top thirties designer, dies.
Siege at Waco, Texas, ends with seventy-six cult members dead. Bomb damages World Trade Center.	Tom Ford appointed design director at Gucci. Tommy Hilfiger launches range of tailored menswear. Elizabeth Hurley causes a sensation in Versace's safety-pin dress.
Channel tunnel opens, linking Britain and France. O. J. Simpson murder trial.	John Galliano appointed head designer at Givenchy. Jean Muir dies. Paul Smith True Brit exhibition, London.
Earthquake destroys much of Kobe, Japan. Poison gas attack on Tokyo train kills ten. Bomb wrecks Federal Building, Oklahoma City. Collapse of Barings Bank, London.	John Galliano takes over the House of Dior. Alexander McQueen replaces him at Givenchy. Hubert de Givenchy retires. Narciso Rodriguez designs dress for Carolyn Bessette's wedding to John F. Kennedy, Jr. Hilfiger launches Tommy perfume.
Outbreak of BSE ("mad cow disease") in Britain. Global warming reaches record high. Atlanta hosts Olympic Games: terrorist bomb kills one and injures 110 at a concert.	Stella McCartney appointed head designer at Chloé. Martin Margiela appointed to design ready-to-wear collection at Hermès. Marc Jacobs appointed designer at Louis Vuitton. Gianni Versace shot dead: sister Donatella takes over. Christie's New York holds sale of Princess Diana's dresses.
Dolly, first cloned sheep, born in Scotland. Massacre of sixty tourists in Egypt. Forest fires in Indonesia cause massive pollution throughout Southeast Asia. El Niño causes damage in South America and southern U.S. Tobacco industry forced to pay billions to cancer sufferers.	Isaac Mizrahi closes his studio. Launch of Prada Sport. Sydney Fashion Week added to fashion calendar.
Hurricane Mitch kills 9,000 in Caribbean. Earthquake in Afghanistan kills 5,000. European Union confirms new currency—the euro.	Alber Elbaz appointed artistic director of Saint Laurent women's ready-to-wear. Bill Blass retires. Issey Miyake announces retirement, appointing Naoki Takizawa his successor.
Earthquake in Turkey kills 15,000.	

Glossary

Armani, Giorgio (b. 1935) Italian designer. Formed his own label in 1975. Famous for suits and jackets, especially the wide-shouldered look for executive women.

Benetton North Italian family firm established in the early sixties by Lucian Benetton. Popular for colorful casual wear and knitwear separates.

Burberry Company founded by Thomas Burberry (1835–1926) in Dorking, England, manufacturing gabardine rain- and sportswear.

Boss, Hugo (d. 1948) German menswear designer. Company achieved prominence in the eighties with suits worn by characters in *Dallas* and *LA Law*.

Comme des Garçons Label formed in 1969 by Rei Kawakubo (b. 1942). His designs attract attention by their muted colors and radical approach to cutting and shaping.

Couture Abbreviation of *haute couture*, which originally meant individually created garments. Now generally used to refer to limited editions of designer clothes.

Dolce and Gabbana Domenico Dolce (b. 1958) and Stefano Gabbana (b. 1962), Italian design partnership. Launched first collection in 1986. Sexy, characteristically Italian aesthetic.

Galliano, John (b. 1960) British designer. Innovative, ultra-romantic, and often quirky, Galliano became one of the top designers of the 1990s.

Gaultier, Jean Paul (b. 1952) French designer. Started his own company in 1977. Now one of the most influential of the French ready-to-wear designers.

Gigli, Romeo (b. 1951) Italian designer. Formed his own company in 1983. His "Italian Madonna" look of 1984 brought him widespread acclaim.

Gucci Italian brand, originally specializing in luxury leather goods and accessories. In 1995, ready-to-wear clothing line appealing to jet-set launched by American Tom Ford.

Hamnett, Katherine (b. 1948) British designer. Established her own business in 1979, particularly successful in Italian and British markets. Famous for large-slogan T-shirts and environmentally friendly cottons.

Hilfiger, Tommy (b. 1951) American self-taught designer. His complete lifestyle collections for men, women, children, and the home reflect a combination of the classics and latest fashion trends.

Jacobs, Marc (b. 1963) American designer. Radical, funky chic. Marc, a diffusion line launched 2001, became a must-have label for young urban hipsters.

Kamali, Norma (b. 1945) American designer. Formed her own label in 1978 and remained popular throughout 1980s and 1990s for fashionable sportswear and office wear for the executive woman.

Karan, Donna (b. 1948) American designer. Worked for Anne Klein until forming her own label in 1984. Renowned for lifestyle collection and stylish casual clothes for the mature woman.

Kenzo (b. 1940) Japanese designer. Worked under his own Jap label in Paris from 1970. Blending Eastern and Western styles, Kenzo paved the way for the wider popularity of Japanese designers.

Klein, Calvin (b. 1942) American designer. Started his own business in 1968, initially specializing in suits and coats but later adding underwear and lifestyle collections. His smooth, understated look typifies modern American design.

Kors, Michael (b. 1959) American designer. Started own womenswear label 1981, producing luxury classics and sportswear. In 1997 appointed head at Céline.

Lagerfeld, Karl (b. 1938) German designer, based in Paris. Launched his own company in 1984 but also worked with Chloé, Krizia, Fendi, and Chanel. His imaginative and witty designs remain a major fashion force.

Lauren, Ralph (b. 1939) American designer. Launched his own label in 1972 and his "Prairie" look in 1978. Classic casual wear in quality fabrics made him a cult designer for the 1980s yuppie buyer and he continues to hold this position.

McCartney, Stella (b. 1972) British designer. Appointed creative director at Chloé in 1997. Collections marked by clean lines and delicate sexy, feminine pieces in mid-1990s bohemian chic style.

McQueen, Alexander (b. 1969) British designer. Worked for Romeo Gigli in Milan before graduating from Central St. Martins, London, when Isabella Blow bought his entire student collection. Provocative and controversial collections disguise exquisite tailoring skills. Appointed chief designer at Givenchy in 1996.

Mizrahi, Isaac (b. 1961) American designer. Started own company in 1987. Chic, sophisticated but youthful clothes in classic American tradition. Switched to a media career in 1998.

Miyake, Issey (b. 1935) Japanese designer. Worked in Paris from 1965 and in New York from 1969; formed own label in 1971. Extremely influential in the 1980s with his bold cutting and draping, and innovative use of textures and sculptural shapes.

Montana, Claude (b. 1949) French designer. Worked in jewelry and leather before launching own-name clothing collection in 1977. Great flair with sportswear as well as leather.

Ozbek, Rifat (b. 1953) Turkish-born British designer. Known mainly for use of eclectic ethnic influences, unusual combinations of fabrics and bright color, although his White Collection of 1990 marked a change to sport-based casuals.

Prada Italian fashion house, developed from leather goods company in 1980s by Miuccia Prada, granddaughter of the founder. Famous for ready-to-wear and accessories, Prada appeals to the fashion elite and celebrities as well as the teen target market.

Westwood, Vivienne (b. 1941) British designer. Closely associated with the rise of the punk movement in the 1970s. Continues to produce original and anarchic collections.

Yamamoto, Yohji (b. 1943) Japanese designer. Formed his own company in 1972; showed his first collection in 1976. Achieved fame with his black-and-white garments but began to allow more color in his collections from late 1980s.

Versace Italian fashion house founded in 1978 by Gianni Versace and taken over on his death in 1997 by sister Donatella. Style is decadent European-style glamour crossed with aggressive disco attitude.

Further Reading

Fewer books have so far been published on the nineties fashion than on previous decades, but this is changing. Magazines and films are still excellent sources for further investigation.

Adult General Reference Sources

Calasibetta, Charlotte. *Essential Terms of Fashion: A Collection of Definitions* (Fairchild, 1985)
Calasibetta, Charlotte. *Fairchild's Dictionary of Fashion*, (Fairchild, 2nd ed,1988)
Cumming, Valerie. *Understanding Fashion History* (Chrysalis, 2004)
Ewing, Elizabeth. *History of Twentieth Century Fashion*, revised by Alice Mackrell (Batsford, 4th ed, 2001)
Laver, James. *Costume and Fashion* (Thames & Hudson, 1995)
O'Hara Callan, Georgina. *Dictionary of Fashion and Fashion Designers* (Thames & Hudson, 1998)
O'Hara Callan, Georgina. *The Encyclopedia of Fashion and Fashion Designers* (Thames & Hudson, 1996)
Peacock, John. *Men's Fashion: The Complete Sourcebook* (Emerald, 1997)
Peacock, John. *Fashion Accessories: The Complete 20th Century Sourcebook* (Thames & Hudson, 2000)
Steele, Valerie. *Fifty Years of Fashion: New Look to Now* (Yale, 2000)
Stegemeyer, Anne. *Who's Who in Fashion*, (Fairchild, 4th ed, 2003)
Watson, Linda. *Twentieth-century Fashion* (Firefly, 2004)

Young Adult Sources

Lomas, Clare. *Twentieth Century Fashion: the 80s and 90s* (Heinemann Library, 1999)

Acknowledgments

The author and publishers would like to thank the following for permission to reproduce illustrations: The Publishers would like to thank the following for permission to reproduce illustrations: Advertising Archive 43bl, 48t, 50t; Arnold Scaasi 37bl; Bath Museum of Costume 30r; B.T. Batsford 35r, 47r, 51l, 56b; Cedars-Erez 36r; Corbis 13r, 34l, 35bl; Gamma 6b; Getty 24l; Getty/AFP 54, 55b: Getty/Time Life 40, 42l; Greenpeace 57; Hanae Mori 14r, 31l; Isaac Mizrahi 39b; Janet Boyes 52r; LA Gear/Heather Rem 22t; Louis Feraud 23r; Norma Kamali 14l; Oscar de la Renta 29r; Rex Features 7, 9t, 10, 12, 13l, 15r, 16, 17, 18, 19, 20r, 21r, 23l, 24r, 25, 26, 29l, 30l, 31r, 33, 34br, 39t, 42r, 43r, 44, 45, 46, 47bl, 48b, 49l, 52l, 53, 56t; Sipa Press 6t, 21l; Spiegal Inc 36l; Topfoto 9b, 15l, 20l, 22b, 27, 28t, 32, 34tr, 35tl, 37tl, 37r, 38, 41l, 43tl, 47tl, 49r, 50b, 51r, 58, 59; Victoria & Albert Museum 8, 24c, 28b, 41r, 55t

Key: b=bottom, t=top, l=left, r=right

Index

Figures in *italics* refer to illustrations.